Praise from readers of James D. Russell's *Beyond the Rim*

"... a moving, instructive and entertaining book. To me as a German reader it offers a rare opportunity: It allows us to get close to an impressive person - an individual who was denied all individuality by the legal, government-approved crime of slavery. *Beyond the Rim* contains a well balanced mixture of a biographical story and personal recollections on one hand and enlightening historical insights on the other hand. The author´s writing is full of spirit and humour, enlivened by colourful anecdotes and brightened by a loving heart."
   -Dr. Hildegard Kurt, Berlin, Germany

"Mr. Russell has the true ability of a fine story-teller. Beyond the Rim takes you to a time and place where you feel the presence of that period....an enjoyable read of true history."
   -Evans Banks, Chicago

"I came to Sperryville to get a copy of your book....I started reading it and could not put it down. I thoroughly enjoyed every word of it. I grew up in Sperryville. I remember Caroline Terry very well. As young boys, several of us would stop by her house and she would tell us stories of the slavery days and Civil War....One thing I do remember is she would laugh and say, 'I outlived all my owners!'"
   -Robert Sealock, Fairfax, Va.

"James D. Russell is a master storyteller. He takes a family story of struggle, tribulation, civil war, and hardship, and makes it a triumphant account of love, honor, vision, and achievement against the odds. Although unique in its features, Beyond the Rim still imparts a history common to us all: the desire for freedom and the loving support of family."
   -Gail S. Lowe, Ph.D., historian, Smithsonian's Anacostia Museum and Center for African American History and Culture

D1453534

BEYOND THE RIM:
From Slavery to Redemption in Rappahannock County, Virginia

•

By James D. Russell

Blackwater Publications

Blackwater Publications
Boston, Virginia
2005

BEYOND THE RIM

Copyright © 2003
by James D. Russell

ISBN 0976452812

Library of Congress Catalog Number 2005922067

Revised edition, 2005

Published by
Blackwater Publications
P.O. Box 80
Boston, VA 22716
www.blackwaterpublications.com
(540) 987-9536

Edited and photographs by James P. Gannon

Designed by Michele Snider
www.msniderdesign.biz or (540) 829-5281

Dedicated to the memory
of Caroline Terry, 1833-1941.

ACKNOWLEDGMENTS

To begin with, I wish to express my sincere appreciation and thanks to Diana Byrd for her invaluable aid in helping me in the structuring of this work. She helped give order to some highly disorganized ideas, not to mention grammar and spelling. She gave of her time, expertise and patience in making "Sis-tah Cah-line" a reality. For this, I say many, many thanks.

I shall always be indebted to James P. Gannon, a retired newspaper journalist and owner of the Old Sperryville Bookshop, for without his guidance and direction this book would have been left unfinished and unpublished. He took time off from his busy schedule to visit the old plantation grave sites, the abandoned school, the old store and other historic places mentioned in the book and pictured in the photographs he took for this publication. He spent many hours editing the manuscript and conducting interviews with me on local history. Above all, Mr. Gannon recognized the merit and local historical significanse of the narrative and continued to encourage the development of this work to its completion. Finally, I would also like to thank Pamela Owen and Mary Hoffherr, who assisted in typing and making the manuscript ready for publication.

Now, as you meander through the pages of historical experience may you find a reason to say, "Thank you, Sis-tah Cahline, for inspiring this story and sharing your piece of American history with us."

Respectfully,
JAMES D. RUSSELL, her great-grandson.

Table of Contents

Caroline Terry was born into the world of slavery sometime in 1833, in Virginia. Andrew Jackson was in the White House as America's seventh president. The United States was a mere forty-four years old. The great event of her life, the Civil War, was eighteen years in the future.

It is not certain just where she was born, but sometime early in her life, Caroline was traded to a plantation owner in the area of Culpeper and Rappahannock Counties. As she matured into a woman, Caroline lived and worked on at least two different plantations in Rapphannock County, a scenic, rural area on the eastern slopes of the Blue Ridge Mountains. Rapphannock became her home. Here she would live, as slave and free woman, for 108 eventful years.

During her long life, Caroline bore six children. The first three were so-called "plantation children", the offspring of slavery's badly kept secret, the union of plantation master and slave. Theodore was born before the Civil War, in 1858; Jennie was born in the final months of that war, in 1865, and Florence was born soon after the war, in 1868. Later, Caroline bore two sons: Daniel, known as "Tony," born in 1873, and Hiawatha, known as "Watha," born in 1874. The sixth child, a daughter named Anne Elizabeth, who was known as "Nannie," was born in 1881.

This historical narrative is based on Caroline's recollections of events as related to the author, her great-grandson, then a 12 year old boy eager to learn what went on during those olden days. I have re-created scenes and conversations consistent with Caroline's recollections as told to me, to capture the spirit, humor and color of her fascinating memories. I have also used my imagination, and my understanding of black people's lives in those days, to create scenes and dialogue that fleshes out Caroline's life story, as might be done in any historical novel.

To listen to this ancient lady answer my questions was to walk through history. Though somewhat reluctant to talk at times of the harshness of her life, she did render a personal account that only she would know. Her favorite snack was a cup of black coffee and a slice of white bread with butter. Not once do I recall her eating cornbread. And the reason she gave was that "the days of cornbread were over" and she enjoyed the days of "eating white bread now." This was a popular post-Civil War expression among the newly freed slaves that is

Caroline Terry, alert and active at the age of 101, sits on the front porch of her little home in Sperryville. She often sat on the porch listening to the music from the nickelodeon at the Celeste Cafe next door. This photo was taken in the summer of 1934.

almost never heard in modern day conversation.

I feel fortunate to have known her. To listen person to person, to touch the gnarled hands, to fetch a cold drink of water or the clay pipe, to help tie the apron, all were opportunities to experience history itself.

Please read and enjoy these notes of treasured memories with me. I believe it is time for me to show how "Sis-tah Cahline," as she was known, endured living "within the rim" of the antebellum plantation, and eventually found a world without fences.

"Beyond the Rim" is a narrative of the plantation life of a slave and her story after liberation. Caroline was my great-grandmother. Because she lived so long, I knew her well and heard her stories many times before her death on July 12, 1941. Her story is important because it demonstrates how recently our nation has put the disgrace of slavery behind us and it may explain why some of our problems related to race and class remain serious to this day.

JAMES RUSSELL
Sperryville, Virginia, October, 2002

PART ONE:
HOW IT ALL BEGAN

A beautiful full moon began its leisurely trek toward the western rim of hope one late spring evening of 1833. Even the warm wind seemed to signal a new beginning as it flowed through the sprawling slave quarters on the plantation. Children played as children do at that age, when thoughts of chains, eternal bondage and servitude were several years away.

As the ritual of the evening meal came to a close, the children were charged with putting by the leftovers, some of which were placed in the cupboard, and these quite often became the warm-overs for breakfast. Milk, pearl tea and other juices were carried to the spring box in the nearby woods. There the cool spring water, as it oozed from the ground, became the only source of refrigeration. Newly picked strawberries, or cherries in a small bowl of milk, were a delicacy. This was a period of welcome respite. After a long, hard day, the victuals in the cupboard provided comfort.

Spring generally brings a renaissance of thought, spirit and an escape from the doldrums of winter months. What did it mean for the slave quarters? The thought of a longer day, the sun in all its glory and more thoughts of going "beyond the rim," the term applied to the boundary lines of the plantation. Severe punishment and the thoughts of additional tasks under the full moon all helped to dispel attempts of going beyond the rim. However, the "grapevine" continued to tell of life "up north" in Canada and the wearing of dressed-up clothes like other people. What if...? How could...? How soon...? Personal thoughts just would not go away. Seasonal change left such thoughts hanging heavily over the quarters just like the full moon.

"Joshua, wha is yo at boy?" This loud inquiry broke the stillness of the quiet cluster of boys who had gathered in front of the drab slave cabin to discuss the meager events of the day. For the moment, Joshua briefly hesitated, but remembering the punishment he received for his previous breach of conduct, replied in his best voice, "Heah ah is, Mama, I'se coming in now." Waiting at the door was a tall, slender, figure with a commanding voice. "Joshua, ah wants yo to go fetch Aunt Lizzie and tell her to git heah rite away. Suki needs her bad."

"Yes'm, Ah'll go lak de wind." Barefoot, in tattered clothes, Joshua took off toward the cabin that housed the local midwife. Enroute he could hear the deep-throated chu-rump, chu-rump of the frogs from the nearby ponds. "Jes wait til tomorrow, ah will get ol Big Eyes, sho-nuf, jes wait n'see." After a short run he reached the cabin of Aunt Lizzie. After knocking at the unpainted door he was admitted to state his mission. "Mama say, please cum up to the house cuz Suki needs yo awful bad." Aunt Lizzie remembered the two women who shared the cabin on the other end of the corridor; Drucilla and Suki were alone because the men in the house had been sold last fall. Joshua looked around the room with its assortment of roots, herbs, sassafras, and pinecones. In addition, the aroma of fat back, collard greens and vinegar filled the room. Aunt Lizzie donned a fresh apron and told Joshua if he would tote her bag, they would get there much quicker.

Off they went, the two of them trudging upgrade toward another great event of the quarters. Upon arrival, Aunt Lizzie quickly took command. The imminent birth of a new baby required the help of someone. Joshua was excused immediately and sent over to the next-door neighbor for the remainder of the evening. The moon in its brilliance continued to bathe the countryside. The wait, the preparation, and finally the gift of God brought joy and relief. Smiles and exclamations of happiness extended as Sis-tah Cah-line made her entry into a world of beauty, pain and uncertain destiny. To the young people, here was another "squeeler." To the elderly, another person was thrust into a cruel environment, unable to live except at the direction of others.

Five years after the arrival of Sis-tah Cah-line, plantation routine was practically unchanged. Crops were planted and harvested and slave discontent remained the same. The one event that could be remembered along with Caroline's birth was the Nat Turner insurrection. Not too many miles away, an attempt by one slave to stage an organized revolt drove home to the white population the unhappiness of the slaves, and their desire to be free. This tragic uprising resulted in the death of more than fifty whites.

Nat Turner was subsequently apprehended and executed. As the story goes, all the slaves on the plantation where Caroline lived were assembled and strongly lectured against any similar uprising or revolt. As for Caroline's mother, Suki, how could she take flight with a baby in her arms? Nevertheless, they were all herded into a cluster by men on horseback with shotguns and threatened death if any such idea ever surfaced.

The years rolled on and inevitably duties increased. Soon

Caroline was a young lady of eighteen when her outspoken personality became known among the quarters. She usually was assigned to help her mother with the laundry. However, on one occasion she was detailed to work in the kitchen in the "Big House." She and another girl, Maudy Bell, were told to report to Miss Emma, the head cook, a fat Aunt Jemima type.

The first morning was routine, cleaning the pots, pans and whatever other duties they were assigned. Later after the work was caught up, they returned to quarters. There, they were beset with questions. Did you see Felicia? Was she really pretty and what kind of clothes did she wear? And above all, did she put on airs just because she was a "high yellow" (mulatto) living in the Big House? The next day brought some interesting and startling answers.

Caroline and Maudy Bell again were called to help Miss Emma. Maudy Bell was detailed the job of picking chickens that Uncle Bledso had placed there for them to finish up in preparation for the dinner meal. Caroline was washing the breakfast dishes when a tall and fair-complected mulatto of perhaps 20 years strode into the kitchen. Felicia's long hair and acqualine nose were in dramatic contrast to the other slave girls performing the kitchen chores.

"Miss Emma, I see you found some blackberries. Did you find both of them in the same patch?" A half-smile crossed the young woman's beautiful face. "Blackberry! Blackberry!" Slowly Caroline realized she was being ridiculed by this house wench. Caroline grabbed a rolling pin from the table drawer and with eyes blazing, declared, "I'll show you what a blackberry is like, I will make you black like me."

Aunt Emma quickly moved toward the impending disaster. "Cah-line, put that pin down. She was jes kidding, like she allas do. Dis is my kitchen and don't mess it up." Felicia retreated up the back stair that led to her room. There in privacy, she realized this Caroline was a girl who did not accept the kidding that the others felt they had to take. Downstairs in the kitchen, Uncle Bledso and Maudy Bell got on either side of the infuriated Caroline. Slowly they walked her back to the quarters.

"Cah-line, that girl Felicia always kids other girls like dat. We is all in the same boat. Some is jus worked in different ways." Caroline, still fuming about the insult, shouted, "Well she's still gotta show me what she means by blackberry patch." Caroline returned to the laundry room and told her mother what happened. The two agreed to talk more about it later. Suki and her daughter later that evening sat down on the stoop in front of their cabin and tried to sort out the events of the day.

"Cah-line, What yo has don gone thru is exactly what the folks in the Big House wants," her mother explained. "Effen the darkey folks is allus stirred up agin each other, den dey can't organize, or help each other to go outside de rim. You gonna find out dat Felicia is really good on the inside, it's jes cuz she is real light lookin, she uses it to live a little easy. Her mother, she light too, an' she was the favorite of the Big House Lady, an she help in de house all de time till Massa had that bad luck and sold her way down South. Miss Emma and her gonna come down here an 'splain mo bout de Big House after de party is over dis weekend."

Caroline promised her mother she would behave and not cause any more trouble "effen that Felicia, with her vanilla self, would keep her mouf shut an neva mention another word bout any blackberry patch."

Finally the day of the "Big To-Do" arrived. Uncle Bledsoe and his helpers had groomed the beautiful lawn, tidied up the flowers around the fence and once again gave it another coat of gleaming white paint. Caroline felt the excitement too, as she once again was going to help in this her first Big House assignment of the Summer Social Series. She had carefully ironed the uniform Miss Emma gave and tried to remember how to serve the guests graciously and promptly. The aroma of freshly baked pies, roast beef, and newly cut flowers permeated the air. Caroline entered the rear yard and paused to look at the fence. She thought for a moment: Big House, Big Folks, Big Money. Behind her down the lane were buildings, bodies, and bondage. Just for a moment, she thought, what a 24-hour day could be like on this side of the fence.

Felicia was at the front door to take the ladies' wraps and to attend their needs as the "Big House Lady" directed. Dinner began amid laughter and conversation of the '49 Gold Rush. One of the guests announced that he was joining the men on the next morning for California. This broad shouldered gentleman arose and announced a toast that for hospitality received he would return with a bag of gold for the entire household. As an afterthought, he added, "You know what? For that black gal that brought in those beautiful biscuits, I am even going to give her a full bag." Caroline felt the blood rush to her face as eyes and laughter were directed at her. She wondered, was she blushing? How prophetic were his words, for sixteen years later in 1865, the gold-seeker's wife did give her a full bag of flour, her very first food as a freed person. The evening passed without incident. Everyone was pleased, and Miss Emma was ecstatic. Caroline had performed well on her first important assignment.

Later the next day, Miss Emma and Felicia paid a surprise visit to the Quarters with a laundry basket carried between them. The basket was laden with leftovers-cake, pies and even a portion of sliced beef, along with peas and mashed potatoes. The sight of Felicia entering the cabin of Caroline and her mother Suki drew a gang of children curious to see the lady that was a part of them, yet apart from them.

"Cah-line, I really wanted to come down before, but this is the best opportunity yet. Though I stay in the Big House, the folks there feel I might try to help someone to escape beyond the Rim. The other week, perhaps I did say things that didn't sound so nice. No more like that I promise. We are all in the same boat together... just have different places. My job is to see that the Missus is attended to for all her needs. 'Felicia, go fetch me a cold drink from the kitchen... go get me my glasses from the parlor... By the way, check the linen in the front bedroom, make sure it's nice and clean...' All day long, it's 'Felicia...Felicia.'"

"My bedroom is at the end of the hall over the kitchen. You know what happens? When the Lady goes to Richmond to shop, the Master then comes to my room - not to shop, but take what he feels like is already paid for. What can I do? What can I say? However, I do listen. There's this man, Lloyd Garrison, Mrs. Beecher Stowe and others. It's something going to happen and it's rolling on toward change without stopping."

Miss Emma, Suki, Maudy Bell and Caroline all sat spellbound, as Felicia talked on, not stammering, not pausing, using big words just like the other folks. Suddenly Caroline took Felicia's hand in hers and held it closely. Then the two of them embraced in a gesture of understanding. Two women, somewhat dissimilar in appearance yet so alike in a common alliance against a disgraceful social order. To Miss Emma and Suki, the sight of a spontaneous togetherness brought tears of understanding. Felicia and Miss Emma left to return to the

Big House. "Cah-line, next time we come down I will tell you about Box Brown of Richmond."

With that, they said their goodbyes. "Bye, Nilla" said Caroline. "Bye Berry" said Felicia. Then time and distance began to separate the two former adversaries.

The summer sun gradually nudged the long hours into days. And slowly the days became weeks. August, one half gone, still the oppressive summer heat continued unabated, save for an occasionally late evening thunderstorm. Caroline and Maudy Bell quite fortunately drew the task of doing the laundry from the Big House's unexpected guests - sheets, bolsters, pillowcases and towels. Suki let the girls take the laundry to the river as it did not require much scrubbing. With laundry basket carried between them in a swinging motion, they walked to the riverbank.

This spot, a medium distance from the quarters, was known as the "wash hole." A fairly long rock, large enough to walk on or to place the wooden tub, jutted into the water, allowing the women to sit and dangle tired feet into the cooling stream. After the chore of washing and rinsing was done, the girls sat on the rock and playfully dipped their feet in the water.

"Does you know what I'se thinking?" Maudy Bell asked Caroline.

"Ah spec I'se thinking de same thing," Caroline replied.

"But, Cah-line, you ain't moving none."

"Hee, hee, but Maudy Bell yo' is." With that, a nudge by Caroline sent Maudy Bell sprawling into the river.

"Ah gits you, you she-devil!" Maudy Bell struggled to stand amid the swirling skirts and soggy blouse. "Gimme a hand, so ah kin get out."

Caroline extended a hand while trying to balance herself

on the flat rock. Maudy Bell grabbed the extended hand, but instead of trying to get out, pulled back with all her might, and suddenly both girls were splashing, giggling, and enjoying a cool dip on a hot August afternoon. "Effen we take dese clothes off, we could dog paddle real good," Caroline suggested.

Both girls removed the waterlogged clothes and placed them on the bushes beyond the rock. Maudy Bell said, "Ain't nothing to worry 'bout, today is Thursday and nobody comes up here dis time of day." On this day, however, it happened that unexpected guests came from the Big House. They had heard of the wash hole and wanted it included on their trail ride. The group led by Felicia, included Mr. Charles, his fiance and Victor and his fiance.

Still splashing and waiting for their clothes to dry, Caroline and Maudy Bell abruptly became aware that they were not alone. They looked up from the water and saw five riders on horseback smiling and observing the afternoon romp. "Well, look what we have here, September Morn", Victor said in a loud voice. Felicia thought to herself: "Black bottoms on parade, what a spectacle."

Charles said, "The one trying to hide is a Venus de Milo". Caroline, still trying to keep in the water at neck level, excitedly replied, "Naw Suh, ah is Cah-line and I doesn't know no Venus."

Laughter erupted from all five onlookers. The two female riders said, "All right enough show, and you men stop looking at those girls." Felicia dismounted and retrieved the girl's underclothing from the nearby bushes and threw them to the embarrassed figures struggling to keep as much as possible submerged. "You girls run home and get dry clothes and then come back for your laundry," she instructed. Caroline realized that Felicia was on their side after all.

Soon the two bathers were on the flat rock after trying to dress partially in the water. "Go ahead, girls, get moving now!" said Felicia sharply. The two broke into a run. The two men watched the retreating figures until they rounded the bushes out of sight. Maudy Bell and Caroline returned to quarters unscathed, feeling relieved that the men's fiancés and Felicia were among the intruders that afternoon.

This latest episode involving Caroline caused quite a stir among the inhabitants of the quarter. The elder folks thought the impromptu swim sans clothes was a welcome signal to "whatever."

Elder One to Elder Two: "You knows how dey is... dey is allus after you wid yo clothes on, and what yo spec when you is without any."

Elder Two: "Sho-nuf honey, but dey say, Felicia she tried to git dem away as quick as she could, so ah don't care what dey say bout her, she can't be all that stuck-up jes cuz she's a high yellow."

Young Gal Number One: "Chile, dey tell me dem gals was hauling heaps of caboose down the cow path, hee, hee, hee."

Young Gal Number Two: "And, boy o' boy, dat Maudy Bell has got a caboose to drag round behind her! Of cose, you kin say Cah-line ain't so bad herself."

Gal Number Three: "What I would had of done effen it be me would be to stoop over rite dere in the sun and pat myself smack on de butt and say you kin kiss it good bye. But, you betta bet ah would make sure ah would be way round the bend out of sight."

Suddenly, Maudy Bell and Caroline appeared. During the course of their evening stroll through the lower quarter, they spied this group of giggling girls and instinctively knew they were the subject of this animated conversation.

"We is de ones, honey, and you had better believe it, we is still running real fast," Caroline said with a smile. The group waved back and watched admiringly, for some of their very own had once again escaped another risk of "whatever."

Several days later, Caroline, Suki, Drucilla and friend Maudy Bell were startled to see two women coming toward their cabin - Felicia and Miss Emma. The sight of this statuesque, beautiful lady brought an immediate halt to the usual cabin chatter. So completely lady-like, even carrying a pink parasol, Felicia was the personification of men's dreams. "Hi girls. Just on a short visit to show you I am keeping my promise to keep you informed on the latest activity at the Big House."

Caroline offered the most comfortable seat in the crude dwelling and listened to the "happenings."

"Remember, I was going to tell you about Box Brown," Felicia reminded them. "Well, listen carefully. Brown was a slave who came up with an ingenious scheme to have himself put in a regular freight box and to be part of a freight shipment from Richmond to Philadelphia. With the help of a Mr. Smithwhite, he was placed in this box and traveled 26 hours until he arrived at his destination. Strangely enough, he was placed in an upside down position for two hours until some alert trainman noticed the direction - This Side Up - and turned the box over. A beautiful story, isn't it? Something is going to happen. It's like the handwriting on the wall, one day we are all going to ride beyond the rim, some going west, some going east, and a lot headed north, and we will be without papers of Manumission."

"OK, girls, got to go. More next time." With that, Felicia arose and waved goodbye. "Bye, Berry."

"Bye, Nilla," replied Caroline with a smile and gesture of

understanding.

The hot days of August slowly ended and life in the quarters gradually shifted into the September-October harvesting of crops and the preservation of foodstuffs for the winter. It was a quiet interlude until the month of November. November, 1860, ushered in an exciting episode for Caroline. Once again the call from the Big House summoned her to work at a social affair. A mantle of fresh snow now covered the drab, foreboding landscape as she trudged forward to the Big House where she was again confronted by unbearable, demeaning circumstances.

The evening meal passed without incident as Caroline did her best to please the Lady of the Big House and her guests. The fireplace was the center scene of folks sitting, talking and enjoying the conversation of the day. Secession, slavery, war, were the topics. When would it come? Caroline tried not to appear too interested yet she listened and took in every word that was said. Mrs. Steptoe, a Southerner of typical views, exclaimed, "What would they do, if they (slaves) were set free? Would the Government give them land and if so, would it be taken from the present landowners? What about schools, should they now be taught as other children, and as they learn, then what?"

The Lady of the House, being a gracious hostess, inquired if any of the guests wanted more coffee or perhaps a bit of wine to help burn the fat. Caroline was dispatched to fetch the demijohn from the cellar so the forum might continue its increasingly lively debate. Mrs. Steptoe demanded mulled wine. Caroline was instructed to prepare the wine for serving.

As Caroline served the wine to Mrs. Steptoe, the woman immediately registered disgust and displeasure. "This gal must have had this wine resting in the snow. Take it back and do as you were told. I requested mulled wine," she demanded. Mrs. Steptoe turned to her hostess and said, "What imbecilic creatures. You just have to take them by the hand and move them like pieces in a puzzle. Oh dear, what a puzzle."

Caroline had been called names before - wench, hussy, bitch - but this term imbecilic creature was something she didn't understand, but she felt it was not in the realm of being human with intelligence. Briskly she retreated to the kitchen where she placed the cup in an already hot oven. From the wood box she tossed in two sticks of sassafras wood, which blazed and added more heat to the stove. After serving more coffee to the other guests she returned to the kitchen for her special project - Mrs. Steptoe's wine. Caroline pulled the overheated mug from the oven and with a touch of fingertips to her lips she then offered a lighting tap to the cup. Her moistened finger sizzled as it touched the overheated cup. "Uh Huh. Mrs. Steptoe, let's see if this will suit your cold, cold, ass."

Then she returned to the dining room, placing the tray of wine and the cups on the carrier and after wheeling it up to Mrs. Steptoe. Caroline retreated to the far side of the spacious dining room to observe the results. Mrs. Steptoe grasped the cup to sample her choice wine. Over-eager flesh and over-heated ceramics met in an exalted collision. "Ouch! This wench is trying to scald me!" screamed the startled Mrs. Steptoe, as she sent the fiery mug crashing to the floor.

"Sally, you must punish that gal immediately! This is uncalled for!" The hostess came forward and tried to make amends.

One of the guests, taking Caroline's side, urged the hostess to do nothing, as Mrs. Steptoe had been a nuisance all evening. "Your gal Caroline did her best to please, and what happened should have happened. So please don't do anything to her."

The hostess said to Caroline, "Go back to the kitchen and remain there until I call you. But before you go, take all this mess and get it cleaned up." Caroline offered her apologies and concern. This was done in her most apologetic manner. But in her Caroline-to-Caroline internal conversation, she expressed satisfaction. "How hot can anyone get without getting burned themselves?"

Surely and swiftly the latest sensation about Caroline reached the quarter's rumor gals.

Gal Number One: "Chile, let me tell you what dat Cahline has done now. Even up dere at the big House she took a bowl of hot wine and threw it in dat ole onery lady's face, yo know, the one what lives in dat special bilt house over on Mud Pike."

Gal Number Two: "And den I heard dat she took up a chair and was gonna bust dat ole critter up side de head effen it had not of been for Miss Sally."

Gal Number Three: "Ah tell you, Cah-line, I don't mess wif her. She will knock yo down, kick yo while yo is falling, and den spit on yo fo God gits de news!"

Thus did the quarter's talk go on until the year ended with the usual Christmas exchange of meager gifts and with dreams of a time when a real Christmas would come.

PART TWO:
THE BEGINNING OF THE END - CIVIL WAR YEARS

The close of 1860 saw the acceleration of tensions between the North and South. The election of Abraham Lincoln as President convinced radical secessionists in the South that leaving the Union was the only way to maintain slavery and the plantation-based economy of the South. This inevitably led to April 12, 1861, the day the Civil War began.

In the last year of growing tensions in 1860 before actual shots were fired, there were four million black men, women, and children under the yoke of slavery. Three million of that number lived in the South. Caroline Terry was just one of them.

The fateful year of 1861 was ushered in on a starlit, cold, sinister New Year's Eve for Caroline, Maudy Bell and all the others in the quarters. They had listened and had heard - now they could feel - something powerful, foreboding, unpre-dictable was in the air.

One powerful force that caused a moral awaking was the novel by Harriet Beecher Stowe "Uncle Tom's Cabin." In this book, the image of slavery became engraved in the minds and hearts of hundreds of thousands of readers. Over one million copies of the book were printed worldwide. Many tears were shed as more people became aware of what was happening in the fields, the work places, and in the dirt floored cabins called homes by people of African descent.

In the writing of one slave who had found freedom, "The slave faces night forever - no dawn of day." There was one white Mississippian who spoke very bluntly: "I'd rather be dead than be a nigger on one of these big plantations."

The icy winter winds of January and February swept the quarters. Drucilla and Suki had covered the earthen floor with sacks that they had saved from the potato and apple storage sheds. Near the windows, rags were stuffed in wherever that biting winter sought to invade. Corn shucks were forced in the airy walls away from the fireplace. How many days until Spring? They marked time by counting the number of beans or dried peas that were added to the jar about the fireplace.

The basic tasks were the feeding of the cattle, and keeping an ample supply of wood for the fireplaces, particularly the ones in the Big House. Slowly the mild winds of March brought a sigh of relief among the black faces along the long corridor of the quarters. The icicles that adorned the medium pitched roofs began their drip, drip, adding to the rivulets that raced toward the meadow beyond. Little black faces sought out the remnants of the melting snow to form the last snow people of the season.

Spring began as no other seasonal change had ever before. Secession was the order of the day. By April the states of Mississippi, Florida, Alabama, Georgia, and Louisiana had left the Union. Virginia came sometime later during the month of May. On April 12 at 4:30 a.m., troops under the command of General Pierre Gustave Toutant Beauregard opened fire on Fort Sumter, near Charleston, South Carolina. The war was on.

Meanwhile, back at the quarters, rumor and speculation ran rampant. News that reached them some days later after the bombardment of Fort Sumter set the quarters ablaze with excitement, including plans to move "beyond the rim" of slavery.

Rumor Gal Number One: "Chile, dey has done started shooting down in South Carolina and all de slaves is gonna go to Washington, D.C. where de President Lincoln is at."

Gal Number Two: "But dey has got dat other President Davis, whar is he at?"

Gal Number Three: "Yo see, dey has done dis heah shooting cuz, the folks down heah wants us to work de plantation, and the folks what lives up North say hit ain't right. So dey done 'lected two Presidents. One who say we is gonna keep on lak we always do. The other President say we is gonna be free to do jes lak de other people is."

Alarmed by events, the plantation owner began to sell many of his slaves as soon as he could. Drucilla and Suki as well as Miss Emma, the cook, remained, as their age limited their trading value. Felicia, on a shopping tour with the lady of the Big House, somehow eluded her mistress and was believed to be heading North. Maudy Bell was sold and separated from her childhood and teenage companion, Caroline.

The overseer came to the quarters again around the first of May and announced that another bunch was due to go to Richmond for auction. He said that the younger the better, for they brought more money. Caroline had already schemed on an escape maneuver, but on second thought decided against it. The auction might actually present an opportunity. She told the overseer: "Take me effen yo wants to, but leave my mammy and Aunt Druie here. Dey can't work no more, dey is worked to death now."

The overseer probably was relieved, for Caroline had become more vocal and difficult every day. This despite the 10 lashes she had received sometime before. The idea of Yankee soldiers on the way gave her just a little more spirit.

The day of the auction came amid reports that if the Yankees came there would be no auction. After demonstration of physical fitness, Caroline was purchased by a land owner from the Culpeper-Rappahannock area. "Glory be" thought Caroline for she now might be reunited with her sister whom she hadn't seen since they were kids.

The evening ride to Culpeper brought tears for she knew that it would be doubtful if she would ever see her mother Suki and Aunt Druie again. Her arrival at the new plantation brought to mind that this was a little better than her other home. The new owners gave Caroline the privilege of having a cabin all to herself. She had been praised as a good cook, sometimes stubborn, but one who could take charge of demanding situations. Later she was to meet Lucy who was about the same age and temperament. Caroline asked, "Why is dey putting me in dis heah cabin by mysef?"

"Honey," replied Lucy, "Dat's what dey call de honeymoon house. In time you will find out."

Still tired from the day's activity, Caroline tossed her small bag of personal items on a chair and immediately fell asleep. Her last thoughts were of what tomorrow might bring. She had been told she would be shown her duties the next day.

The next morning, Lucy gave Caroline an orientation on the peculiarities of her new owners. The master of the house had a severe drinking problem and this prompted the mistress to lock herself in her room on different occasions. This exclusion within the house left the master to wander around with wine flask in hand to cavort among the slave quarters. Lucy went on to explain the "honeymoon house." His personal choice outside the house was housed in the cabin nearby. The wife had threatened to leave but the advent of war and the wealth involved influenced her decision to wait it out and just tolerate her husband's drunken forays.

Caroline and Lucy were in command of the kitchen and the well-stocked pantry and stock room. The weeks went by with no unusual activity. The war came closer and closer. Lucy and Caroline pondered their fate. News of slaves leaving in large numbers to escape to the Yankee-occupied areas became everyday items of gossip and speculation.

The endless days of a country at war with itself began to take a toll on the landowner. His possessions, particularly his slaves, became a dilemma. Fortunately for him, most of his slaves remained on the plantation. They feared falling within the grasp of the Confederate forces and their rumored brutality kept the slaves in place to wait for the Union's overwhelming numbers. In 1862 strange things began to happen on the plantations. As the Union forces advanced throughout the South, slaves fled to the encampments of the northerners. This situation led to a conflict between the Fugitive Slave Act and what was known as "contraband of war" - runaway slaves who fled to the Union army camps.

Union General Benjamin E. Butler's command at Fortress Monroe became the focal point on the question of "contrabands," slaves who came to work on the Union side. The issue became acute when three slaves escaped from work on the Confederate side and made it to the domain of General Butler. Their master pursued them relentlessly and argued that they be returned immediately. Then came a Congressional ruling that gave authority to Union commanders to liberate those slaves who were employed by the Confederate Army.

Caroline and Lucy remained on the plantation although they constantly traded ideas on when and where they would go.

Lucy to Caroline: "Sis-tah Cah-line, dey say that when de slaves is caught, dey are taken out and shot lak dogs."

Caroline replied, "Lemme tell you, Lucy, I don't know jes zackly what to do. You know when I fust come here dat was called de honeymoon house, yo know wha I is at. Well ah has done found out why it's got dat name. Late one evening after all de supper was done, Massa Frank came and banged on mah door. I thot dat Mistress Georgia had don got sick, but he was drunk and had a big wine bottle in his hand. So he say, "Cah-line dat was one stupendous meal. I must pat you on the back for dat. But listen, Lucy, what he was patting on wasn't de

Lucy Starks, Caroline's life-long friend from plantation days as slaves, was pictured in this photo in National Geographic magazine decades ago. Lucy, like Caroline, smoked a clay pipe and did her washing by hand, boiling water over an open fire. Lucy died a tragic death in the mid-1930s when she accidentally set her dress on fire while lighting her pipe.

back, he was patting on de caboose."

Lucy said, "Cah-line, dis is de manner of all menfolks. Dey figgers de Good Lord knowed what he was doing when he made a woman to help old Adam out." Caroline sat patiently as Lucy went on to explain relations between male and female.

The year 1863 was a devastating year of human misery. Gross confusion existed in the matter of currency: Notes were issued by the Confederate Treasury as well as banks, states, private companies, and railroads. The local farmers and plantation owners were requested to contribute one-tenth of their produce to the Confederate army. For the large plantation owner this did not impose a hardship as it did for the small farmer. The plantation owner sought to hold on to his slaves and hundreds were herded like cattle and marched away from the battle area to as far away as Texas. On the other hand, slaves continued to flee toward the Union lines. The losses in income, goods, and food gave rise to a riot in Richmond. Women by the hundreds smashed windows and looted stores for clothing and food. "Blame the Yankees" was the rallying cry.

Meanwhile, the plantation gals shared information, viewpoints and prognostications.

Gal Number One: "Massa Frank say that whenever any of them Yankee soldiers come on his place he is gonna cut off their business."

Gal Number Two: "Honey, effen he do that, den what kind of business is dey gonna be in?"

Gal Number Three: "Heh, heh, dey is just got to have little signs that say de shop is closed, on account we is 'Out of Business.'"

Gal Number One: "You know, that could work down here on the plantations. Just take a look. Did you ever see so many of them funny butter-bean looking niggers? Where they come from? It's been a whole lot of fence-jumping effen you ask me."

Caroline and Lucy continued their close-knit relationship, each confiding on matters of personal dealing with the Big House. Master Frank continued to drink, perhaps a little more openly as the war's economic stress hit his farm. Many planters resorted to bribery to sell their products to the North. For cash, officials on both sides forgot the conflicting issues and looked for profits.

In a late evening stopover at Caroline's cabin, Lucy noticed an unusual change in her friend's attitude and response to questions on the Big House. "Cah-line, you told me bout a year ago bout the drinking boy coming to you cabin, well I spose he still is. Is dat right? Nother thing. Ah see you is putting on mo' weight. Is dis cuz you in family way?"

Caroline confessed. "You remember what I tol you about that high-yellow gal name of Felicia at the other plantation? Well, the same happens to me. Only this fall, whatever is gonna be happening is because of whatever happened a few months ago. I hopes it will be a boy. At least he will have one job to do - not two lak us women has to do."

"Well, Cah-line, while you is having de baby I can keep de kitchen going and help out. It's time now for us to stick together as best we can. We bleed, we breed and we plead, but all dis is gonna change sometime soon. The Yankee folks will make things different as never before."

With that a silence overtook both women as they shared a feeling of mutual aid and trust.

Master Frank had two daughters and they were both aware of the changed climate in Caroline's cabin. They knew the reason, but silence prevailed, an acceptance of unspoken and unacknowledged plantation practices.

From North to South, war rolled on during 1863 and 1864, bringing the conclusion closer and closer. General Lee's Confederates met disaster at Gettysburg, Pennsylvania, while General Grant captured the once-impregnable fortress on the Mississippi at Vicksburg. Hopes of victory began dying in the South.

The war was getting close to Caroline's plantation. En route north for Lee's Pennsylvania campaign, Jeb Stuart and his Confederate troops clashed with Union horse - soldiers in the biggest cavalry engagement of the war. Thousands of men fought on horseback for 12 hours along the Rappahannock River, near Brandy Station - only a few miles from the plantation.

Caroline was now the mother of a beautiful baby boy, a gift of the Big House. The daughters of Master Frank were amazed that the baby was so fair and with a fine texture of hair. The girls, of course, were not encouraged to take any special interest in this offspring; however the sight of one from the cabin with such remarkable likeness completely overwhelmed them.

"Cah-line, let us name the baby, please? May we, please?" "And just what's that gonna be?", asked Caroline in absolute surprise at the girl's interest.

"Theodore shall be his name after our great uncle," said Emily, the eldest of the two teen-aged girls. "All right," replied Caroline, "But is you girls gonna look after him while ah is in de kitchen?"

"Sure we will," the girls said, but both Cah-line and the girls smiled for they knew that it would be doubtful. The girls thought of Theodore as a living doll - and compared him as one of their own. To Caroline, the baby's lack of Negro features seemed strange. Despite being conceived under the most harsh conditions, he would receive love and care and return love.

Caroline reflected on her times of living on the other plantation and of the attention and greater freedom given to Felicia. Felicia had been taught to read and write and Caroline wondered if they would do the same for little "Thea." Then she remembered how the girls tried to correct her for saying "dem" and "yestiddy". Caroline tried, but thought to herself, what is the difference, "dem days" or those days and "yestiddy" and yesterday? In only too short a time all will be the same, a bit of history.

While reminiscing, Caroline thought of an encounter in which she herself almost became history. During the past year, a contingent of Union soldiers stopped by the plantation seeking food and a place to rest. When the plantation owner provided them with home cooked victuals, they ate as if on the verge of starvation. After consuming a good meal, they heaped praise continuously. The lure of the giant shade trees in the oversize yard was the next attraction.

Emily and Angie, her sister, sat at the side of a lily pond, where two large ceramic bullfrogs appeared to be on guard duty. One young Yankee officer, a lieutenant, walked along the edge of the pool to get a better look. "Please do be careful, for those stones might give way," one of the sisters said. "Oh, I could do a jig on these rocks," the lieutenant replied, and with that, hoping to impress the young girls he commenced a high step, arms out stretched. Suddenly a stone fell loose and into the water he fell.

Everyone laughed, for nothing serious happened except a drenching of self-esteem and pride. The young man came out of the shallow pond shaking the water from his uniform when he saw Caroline at the far end of the yard, laughing in unison with the others.

"I will be damned if I will have a nigger laughing at me,"

the Union officer swore. He drew his pistol from its holster and took a few steps toward Caroline. "No! No!" screamed Emily and Angie. Both girls ran and stood between the officer and the speechless slave woman. "Why do you want to kill her, she is a human being and reacted like everyone else here." The lieutenant's comrades reminded him that he had been warned, and the fall into the pool was the consequence of his own misjudgment. The officer was unrepentant. "I know, but if it weren't for those damned niggers, we would not have to be here at all."

Caroline fled to her cabin, shaken to tears at her close encounter with death. This incident occurred, it is believed, about the time of a cavalry engagement between Robertson's Brigade of Confederates and the First Maine Cavalry near Sperryville, Virginia, on July 5, 1862.

The days bore rumors about the various atrocities committed against the runaway slaves. Caroline and Lucy sat alone and pondered the wisdom of following the slaves who managed to escape to the safety of the Union lines. What if the Yankee men were chased back North? Lucy with her traditional reasoning, said, "Honey, dere is the answer dere", as she pointed to little Theodore, "We do have plenty of food, a roof overhead and a baby who for some reason seems lak he belongs in the Big House."

Toward the fall of 1864, conditions on the plantation began to deteriorate. The prospect of a Yankee victory caused the owner to reassess his economic situation in light of the likely outcome of the war. He made an offer to his slaves that in the event of slavery ending, they would be free to go or stay and work on a conditional basis.

But that was in the future. In the meantime, the war presented some urgent tasks. One of them was to bury the dead after the battles. At one point, Caroline and Lucy, along with other slaves, were loaded into wagons and transported to the scene of a recent battle. It would become a memory deeply impressed into her mind, even into old age.

Lucy and Caroline were given shovels to help the menfolk who actually did the hard work with picks and digging bars. Caroline tried to help as directed but owing to her pregnant condition she was limited. The Rumor Gals at the plantation had been noticing and commenting, as usual.

Gal Number one: "See, I told you she was gone again."

Gal Number two: "What you spect, dat man aint keeping her in de honeymoon house fo nothing."

Gal Number Three: "Well, lak dey say, once you start stirring dat chocolate up de richer it gits, ha-ha."

Caroline was now carrying the second "gift of the Big House." As the war and its economic stress increased, so did Master Frank's consumption of "lip-lap," as they called liquor then. This meant more stop-bys and stay-overs at the honeymoon house. So now the pregnant Caroline walked on the battlefield amid the corpses, carrying a shovel. She and Lucy came upon the stiff body of a young Yankee officer. She could not be sure, but Caroline believed it could be the one who wanted to shoot her in the lily-pond incident almost two years earlier. A pistol and a pair of binoculars lay at his side. Caroline thought to herself: Everyone knew she was a little bit pregnant. So if she could hide the pistol and binoculars under her clothing she would be just a little more pregnant. She thus concealed them and took them home. The pistol became one of the family's enduring souvenirs of the Civil War. (It remains in the author's possession even to this day, a priceless reminder of "Sister Cah-line" and her times.)

As the war progressed, the plantation owner began to talk

to Caroline more of his losses on the plantation and to repeat his promise to free all slaves when the time came at the end of the war. His conduct became more blatant and open as the year came to an end. On one early morning visit he cursed and began raving because he could find no more to drink.

He started to fling the empty wine flask into the fireplace when Caroline said, "Jes a minute, I wants to show you something. Effen you looks in the bottle you won't see nothing but the bottom-all gone, nothing left but a bad taste. Jes look out the window - all the dead mules and soldiers are all gone now and de sun is coming up pretty and red, lak always. De snow will soon be coming and will wash away all de bad things and den the spring will bring flowers as never before. If you jes always look at the bottle you will see nothing more than the empty bottom when de liquor is all gone. Now when yo looks out de window long enough, de whole field changes from

This is the colt revolver that Sister Caroline picked up the battlefield while on burial duty.

snow to warm days, to flowers and then de leaves puts on their show. It is a long road that doesn't turn sometime and somewhere."

Massa Frank replied in a drunken stupor, "What in the hell makes you so smart?"

Caroline responded, "Ah has been on a long, long road for a long, long time and now it's bout to turn."

Without another word the master turned, and slowly dropped the empty flask on the bed and strode out the door. Only once more did he visit the cabin, and that was the following spring of 1865. Caroline, Lucy and Baby Thea went about the daily routine as much as possible. Jeffrey, Lucy's brother, was now a part of the clan. For some reason Massa Frank saw to it that he would stay. Caroline and her son Thea stayed in the honeymoon house. Carefully hidden away were the binoculars, pistol and the discarded wine flask.

On the battle front many Confederate soldiers were deserting because of poor rations, lack of supplies and battle losses. The dreadful days of the winter 1864-1865 came to an end that saw the Union forces flush out the remnants of the Confederacy. Petersburg no longer remained a stronghold; the entire area was now a vista of death and destruction.

General Grant's Union troops broke through Petersburg on the march toward Richmond. April 1 to April 5 were crucial days in the War Between the States. Chaos was unleashed in Richmond. The retreating Confederates set fire to a great portion of the city. Mobs looted the stores and shops in a frenzied effort to secure what food was left. Richmond fell to Union occupation. The Northern soldiers were greeted by dancing slaves who sang, cried and beat on tin pans and pots in an ecstatic display of emotion. April 3, a day to be known as glory day, began as President Lincoln entered the conquered city. Former slaves, weeping for joy, hailed him: "I know I am free. For I have now seen Father Abraham and have touched him." President Lincoln deflected their praise and thanks. "You must kneel to God only, and thank Him for your freedom."

On the plantation, Caroline and Lucy sang praises and prayed for happiness or rather offered a prayer of Thanksgiving for this was indeed happiness. They then joined the other slaves in a day and night of celebration.

On Sunday, April 9, 1865, General Lee surrendered the remnants of his defeated army to General Grant at Appomattox Courthouse. On the plantation, Caroline and Lucy joined in the continuing the dancing and celebration.

The livestock and poultry joined in their own way, too, with a pig or two becoming an impromptu barbecue, and several chickens contributing to the feast. Several cases of wine, or demijohns somehow showed up on the menu. Jeffrey, Lucy's brother, and another ex-slave called "Wingy" were the main entertainers in the dance of the century. If the banjo player or the fiddler became exhausted, then a huge ring of hand clappers and foot stompers went into action. It was a rhythmatic hand beat with the lone dancer in the center of a huge ring. Here Wingy, a tall muscular fellow, excelled in what was called "Falling off the Log," a fast-paced dance of fancy footwork. After Wingy, came Jeffrey in the "Turkey Trot" and what was probably the forerunner of the "Back Bay Shuffle."

After a day or two the plantation owner announced to the remaining ex-slaves a plan for them to stay on and work as paid help. Each farm hand, as they would be called, would have a cabin in which to live free. Also promised were several hundred pounds of flour, a garden space, wood for the fireplace or stove and money at the end of the week with which to buy clothes and other necessary items. It is believed that this was the origin of the term "Year Hand." Further south, other ex-slaves entered into plans called sharecropping. Whatever the plan, the bulk of the remaining ex-slaves stayed on and worked for many, many years to come.

After the celebration had spent itself, Caroline gathered her two children, Theodore in hand and baby Jennie in arms and took a long walk to the edge of the plantation. She sat down on a fallen tree log and pointed toward the boundary line. "See way over there, dats de other side of de fence. You ken go across dere lak the other folks now. No dogs to hunt you down and no whip waiting fo you. Dis is de day of glory!" The Rumor gals had the time of their lives after days of unrestrained frolic.

Gal Number One: "Chile, I'se gwine to the city and git me some fancy clothes."

Gal Number Two: "You know, de way yo stomach has been growling, you best let yo back go fo awhile."

Gal Number Three: "What's yo gonna do, see if dey fits going out the door?"

Gal Number One: "Lemme tell you. Effen dey wants to borrow what I has to lend, I'll have money to burn and some to spend."

And a chorus in response: "Yo is a hussy, sho nuff,"

The month of April was full of tragedy, triumph and upheaval. First came the surrender of Lee's forces at Appomattox. The celebration of victory was underway when President Lincoln's assassination brought mourning throughout the North and among the former slaves. The just-freed people of color felt the grief as no one else did, for they feared that they would be returned to bondage.

Gradually, some degree of order was restored, as Lincoln's successor, President Andrew Johnson, tried to sort out priorities. More confusion and heartbreak lay ahead in the Era of Reconstruction. This postwar effort of about twelve years was designed to provide a transition period for the ex-slaves, including training and developmental process to bring them into political and economic equality.

Back on the plantation, Caroline cared for her three "Big House children," Theodore, Jennie and Florence, the last born in 1868. The four of them moved out of the honeymoon house and into another one on the grounds. However, Theodore - or "Thea" as he was nicknamed-continued to dominate the attention unlike any other Big House children. Until they grew beyond their teen-age years, Angie and Emily taught Thea how to read and groomed him in the ways of a houseboy.

One incident occurred when Thea was inducted in the childhood version of the Ku Klux Klan. Angie in her usual mischievous mood fashioned a comical hat and placed it on Thea's head and said "Look, Emily, here is my little Ku Klux Koon." Laughter erupted as Angie led him in hand around the room. The older persons who had gathered seemed amused at the spectacle and remarked, "at least he is better looking than those other koons".That brought more laughter and another remark, "Thank goodness for something to laugh about."

Caroline and Lucy found themselves wondering which route to take in the future. They were free to go - but where would they go? They were assured by the plantation owner that work was there without going elsewhere. They elected to stay.

Strange things did happen as Caroline was located in her new home. The broad-shouldered man, who had visited the plantation in the past, stopped by and inquired about the black woman who served those delicious biscuits at that time. Now 16 years later, he would keep the promise he made concerning a full bag of gold as a gift. Only this gold was a full bag of flour - the first food given to her as a freed person. She thanked him again and again.

Caroline was still a young woman of childbearing age and now that her association with the honeymoon cabin was over, she began to look for a more sincere and lasting relationship. Jeffrey and Caroline found some solace in each other's company. A mother of three, Caroline began to look to the future. She was no longer faced with the threat of being separated from her children. Mothers and fathers and sons and daughters now could remain together. She began to search for a relationship of some permanency.

Lucy's brother, Jeffrey, and Caroline began their somewhat tumultuous romance in an old outbuilding-the corncrib. The two of them were given the assignment of shelling corn there. Lucy, with her usual intuition, followed the couple at a discreet distance and stood outside listening to the grinding and whirring sound of the hand-cranked corn sheller. As she suspected, silence descended after a while. Lucy retreated to her cabin and calmly prepared to lecture the couple. When Jeffrey and Caroline returned to the cabin, Lucy took off in rare form.

"What I want to know is: How kin you do any corn shelling wifout making any noise? You see dis broomstick heah? Well, it's either going to be something to jump over, or it's going up side of yo heads. Both of you!" (Jumping over the broomstick was a tradition at weddings among the blacks - a sign of commitment.) There was no response from the startled couple. But some months later, Jeffrey and Caroline were married.

The war had left in its wake vast destruction of industry in the South, disruption of farming, and a shortage of manual labor that had been the basis of the plantation economy. In Virginia alone, there were 360,000 idle ex-slaves. In time these were gradually employed as the demand for workers increased and the need for the basic necessities of life drew the idle hands back to the fields and workshops.

Race relations in Virginia were less than ideal, but not as chaotic as in some other states. Federal authorities came south and tried to help the freed blacks in terms of health, education, housing and jobs. Education had been denied the slaves, except in the case of some more enlightened slave owners who recognized the value of being able to read and write.

Slowly, the colored people were integrated into the economy and social order, even into public office. But white acceptance of this change was slow and grudging. The whites feared that the colored would "take over." There had been no time of preparation to bridge the cultural, educational and economic differences that separated the two races. The whites distrusted, feared violence and were generally unwilling to accept the freed blacks.

Much credit is due to the Freedmen's Bureau, created by the Federal government after the war to help the ex-slaves. The Freedmen's Bureau provided over two hundred schools during its existence. It is believed that 50,000 persons of color learned to read and write and to understand the printed word. Northern whites, mostly women, came South to teach the colored who wanted to learn. Gatherings included children and adults, alike eager to learn via the printed word.

Over the years the yearning for learning became an obsession among the freed colored persons. Among some, however, the years of doing without gave a false idea that to have common sense or mother wit was sufficient to live on. This idea gradually faded as the educated colored persons succeeded. The ex-slaves who had gathered to listen to speakers of note left surprised, proud and completely transfixed. It was difficult for them to believe that there were colored individuals who could speak without stammering, without looking at their feet, or scratching their heads and who use words just like whites.

Caroline was among the many who had listened to the new hero, the learned colored man. Of course, the colored preacher became one of the new symbols of influence. He could move his fingers along the printed lines and explain the evils of sin, such as the barrooms, dancing on Sundays, even playing ball on Sunday.

The white teachers who contributed their time to direct the learning of the colored people also spoke on the sanctification of marriage as opposed to sexual promiscuity. Their teaching encouraged the concept of family life - one father, one mother and children under one roof.

Caroline and Lucy, a bit older now and certainly more in charge of their own future, became eager to learn of the religious route to happiness and contentment in a land so bereft of these pursuits for so long. Lucy eventually moved to a new residence where she married and started her own family.

As for Caroline, her romance and eventual marriage to Jeffrey that began as a corncrib encounter began to feel the winds of change. By 1882, Caroline's temperament and Jeffrey's restless nature boiled over into a separation.

However, this did not occur before two sons were born to this union.

Theadore was living at the Big House as houseboy, a much-desired position. Caroline's family now consisted of the Big House children - Thea, Jennie and Florence, and the two younger sons of Jeffrey - Daniel, who was known as "Tony" (born in 1873) and Hiawatha, nicknamed "Watha" (born in 1874). Caroline never learned to read, but she was a good listener. Angie and Emily would take turns in reading to her the Holy Bible, the first priority, and whatever literature the young ladies liked. Among her favorites were books of the "Luck & Pluck" series, and some poetry. Her youngest son's name was suggested by the poem by Henry Wadsworth Longfellow, "Hiawatha."

Another influence on Caroline were the admonishments by teachers from the North on morals and personal conduct. The next move in Caroline's social development was her baptism. Caroline now became a person of Christian faith and respectability. In 1881, her sixth and final child was born, a beautiful baby girl. Her formal name was Anne Elizabeth, but she was always called "Nannie." Baby Nannie completed the family of "Sis-tah Cah-line."

Moving ahead into a new century, in the years 1900 through 1910, Caroline's daughter Florence had married and had three daughters of her own. Jennie also married and eventually became the mother of eight. Watha and Tony later became the parents of two sons and six children respectively. Strangely enough, Thea did not marry but instead parlayed his good looks into romancing a lot of admiring ladies. He would read whatever came his way. An insatiable thirst for information via the printed word characterized him as a mature man. (Another characteristic was an insatiable thirst for fruit of the vine in its fermented state.) Those who did not bother to apply themselves to the printed word he called "boneheads."

During the decade 1910-1920, Caroline and her brood of six children multiplied into several families, some of whom moved out of Virginia. Caroline had become a grandmother, and then a great-grandmother.

PART FOUR:
HOME AT LAST, IN SPERRYVILLE

One of the former slave's goals was to own her own cabin and land. She told of giving seven dollars to a local man as down payment on one egg-shaped acre in Majors Hollow, a settlement for blacks just west of the village of Sperryville. However, her daughter Nannie was able to provide her a home of her own in the village. It was a two-story, four-room house, with no electricity or running water, and a well with a bucket-pull chain in the yard. This modest dwelling remained her home for roughly thirty years until she died.

As an aging lady, Caroline gained standing in the community through her interest in the church and religious gatherings. According to one story, twelve colored members of a local white church held a meeting in the home of "Sis-tah Cah-line" and the result was that the Hopewell Baptist Church was organized. Subsequently the first Hopewell Church building was constructed on a hillside in the village of Sperryville.

New friends entered Caroline's life: Rev. Carey, Uncle Dan, Aunt Harriet, Aunt "Rhett" (Henrietta), Uncle Arthur and Mrs. Daniel, to name a few. There was a close bond among them, for they had emerged from slavery. To survive and improve their lot was a great accomplishment. Although Caroline probably met a great-granddaughter, Martha Anderson, only once in her lifetime, she was ever ready to inform any listener that she had a great granddaughter in college.

As Caroline and her lifelong friend, Lucy, advanced in years, their once lively presence became like that of all senior citizens-quiet, observing and increasingly dependent on close relatives for her well-being. Nannie worked and lived in New York where she had gone as a teenager. Among those who helped watch "Sis-tah Cah-line," and tend to her needs, was the little boy called "Jeems," the author of this chronicle.

Caroline now traveled only rarely and was content to reminisce about the long and stormy road she had traveled. From seeing the fine carriages of yesterday to the fine automobiles of 1940, including some owned by colored people too. Some of the church members would come by and pick her up and take her for a ride. She and Lucy enjoyed this. However, her naming of the airplane was "there goes an air plant." No one laughed or tried to correct. To listen to whatever she said was a treat.

Tony and Watha were the "bad boys" of the town. Tony was not exactly lazy or afraid of working too hard, but it might be said he had some aversion to excessive manual labor. Both men in their youth were regular customers of the Hazel Mountain area where moonshine liquor was a Saturday must. One memorable occasion was the suicide attempt by Uncle Tony. Both men after a visit to The Hazel returned home and began to drink heavily. Caroline and her granddaughter, Roberta, became alarmed and afraid, for Tony began to flash his long barreled pistol that he often carried. "Tony, Tony, please put that gun away and stop that drinking so much" begged Caroline. Watha and Tony continued to imbibe without let up. Tony had an old banjo and laid the gun down to play while Watha would dance around the room. Tony with his banjo picking and Watha who would stop long enough to sing made an unusual floor show.

"Somebody stole my old coon dog.
I wish they's bring him back.
To chase the big hogs thru the gate
and the little ones thru the crack.
Possum up the persimmon tree,
the raccoon in the hollow.
Pretty gal at Massa's house,
so fat she kin hardly wallow.
Well, I can't read a ought
and neither kin I figger,
but, I'se got too much pride to talk to de nigger."

With the last verse, Tony began to search for one more drink. However, while the concert was in full swing, Caroline took the gallon jug and carried it to another part of the house. Watha had fallen asleep from all the song and dance and was completely unaware of the dilemma.

"Mama, what have you and Berta done with my liquor?" Tony asked. Neither woman said anything, but stood silently in the doorway of their bedroom to watch the next show. "You all don't want me to have nothing." With that statement he picked up the revolver and said. "I am going to kill myself and be out of the way."

The next move was Caroline and Roberta running back into the bedroom and locking the door behind them. Tony moved to the yard and sat down with his back leaning on the oaken bucket well. Suddenly the loud report of the gun broke the silence of the evening. "Oh, my Lord, Grandma, Uncle Tony has killed himself." Roberta and Caroline began to hug each other for support. Watha awoke with alarm and wanted to know what was going on. The women were too terrified to look. The three of them went out into the yard where Tony was slumped against the well, his pistol at this side. When they got closer they observed a big hole in the black western hat he always wore. Tony then opened one eye and laughing asked the weeping women, "Did you think I'se gonna do that for sure, I jes did it a little bit." What actually happened was when he sat down by the well, he took his hat off and shot a hole in it and then placed it back on his head. Watha by this time had sobered up and said, "Tony, effen I could find a stick I would bust you up side de head."

Roberta and her grandmother, Caroline, still shaken by the sound of the gun and the sight of the hole in the hat, walked hand in hand to her daughter, Florence's house. They returned later to find all quieted on the home front.

By this time, her advanced age had retired Caroline to the front porch rocker. Nevertheless, for the visitors who came by, she was eager to listen and especially to have someone read passages from the bible to her. To have some of the Hopewell Church members come by for prayer service was the highlight of her retirement.

Her son, Theodore, continued to travel with his ring of friends, all imbibers to be sure. Watha was one who carried a short fuse. Numerous scrapes with the local law enforcement officers kept him a familiar face on late Saturday night round-ups.

Jeffrey, a senior citizen, was still a roadrunner although at a slower pace. Jeffrey had married Caroline after a rather monitored courtship. Jeffrey used his left over charm and persuasive tongue to keep a roof over his head. He kept company with a lady called Aunt Hagger. His usual approach was his urgent need for board and lodging. The next step was to become a star boarder. Next a promise of marriage as soon as one little personal debt was paid. Weeks became months and lo and behold two years came and the first of August 1919, or thereabouts would be three years.

The shade tree in Aunt Haggers' front yard was a favorite of Jeffrey's. In his usual rocker, he was approached by Aunt Hagger who asked, "Jeffrey, is you gonna marry me?" Jeffrey replied, "Marry you, huh no indeed, ah ain't gonna marry

With the beautiful Blue Ridge Mountains as his backdrop, James Russell kneels to examine the gravestone on a farm a few miles south of Sperryville where he believes his great grandmother worked as a slave. The stone marks the graves of James A. Ryan and his wife Elizabeth, who may have owned Caroline for a time. "She was always talking about Marse Ryan," James remembers. It is believed that Caroline was owned by two or three different plantation masters before she became free.

you." Aunt Hagger retreated to the kitchen where she had been preparing a huge pot of water to accompany her marriage request. Armed with the pot of boiling water she again repeated her request for an urgent need to regain a degree of respectability. "Jeffrey, is you going to marry me?" "Woman, I has done tol you no." Having tiptoed to the back of Jeffrey she lifted the pot and let go its entire contents on his back. Jeffrey lept into the air with a scream heard around the hollow. For an agonizing five minutes he ran in circles, arms flailing and finally sat down amid tears, curses and prayers and permitted Aunt Hagger to cut the shirt from his pain-racked body. He remained at Aunt Hagger's, paid his debt and left.

Caroline's comment: "Well, sometimes some of those 'Hot Poppa's' have to get hit on the head more than once before dey learns to do the right thing."

Caroline's friends furnish another humorous episode toward the end of the long journey.

Aunt Harriet reportedly felt some discomfort and sought medical attention from Doctor Smith who rode his horse to the home of his patients as he made house calls. When summoned to Aunt Harriet's home he inquired, "All right Aunt Harriet, what seem to be the trouble?"

"Well, Doctor Smith, ah jes feels so giddy bout the head."

"Aunt Harriet, I wouldn't worry too much about that, all niggers are giddy about the head."

"Well, it started a day or two ago." Aunt Harriet had been reading the Page News and Courier. Dr. Smith noticed this and said, "What's this they are saying about our President Hoover?" As Aunt Harriet handed him the newspaper a copy of Captain Billy's Whiz Bang dropped out.

Captain Billy's Whiz Bang was the 1930 version of Playboy, Penthouse and the like. Dr. Smith laughed and said,

"No wonder you are giddy about the head." Aunt Harriet tried to hide her embarrassment, "Oh, my nephew must have had that while he was reading the paper." Dr. Smith replied, "But it was still in there while you were reading it. Here take these pills for that dizziness and get in touch with me later." Still laughing, "I would not show Danny that for you both might get giddy about the head." (Uncle Danny and wife, Harriet, were both in their eighties.)

What was happening in the rest of the countryside was of great significance in terms of development in the Negro community. President Roosevelt in an effort to revive the nation's economy created what many called "Alphabet Soup." Under his administration, such R.E.A. (Rural Electrical Administration) T.V.A. (Tennessee Valley Authority), W.P.A. (Works Progress Administrations) and quite notable in Virginia was the C.C.C. (Civilian Conservation Corps). This agency gave valuable help in the form of small bridge building, tree planting, etc. Over eighty camps were established in Virginia in 1937, twelve for colored. They also constructed ditches for soil erosion. Young unmarried males were given six months of work, complete with uniforms and meals, lodging and some educational instruction. Six state parks were developed in Virginia. These eventually came under the jurisdiction of the State of Virginia.

The year 1933 began for Caroline as exciting and dramatic as some of her earlier plantation experiences. Theodore, her first-born, as usual contributed to the excitement with his encounters with "Mr. Alcohol." The Civilian Conservation Corps had started working on the Skyline Drive and the blasting of the tunnel near the Panorama Point could be heard in the village Sperryville seven miles distant. Watha was back home after having left almost fifteen years before because of some altercation with the local folks. It was alleged that Watha was involved in an incident somewhere in Arkansas in which a man was seriously injured - probably fatal. Watha was accompanied by a man named Barnes who stayed approximately three days. Barnes gave the story that he was helping Watha get out of Arkansas and home as Watha was having trouble with his eyesight. However, Watha was in his middle fifties. His reputation as a bad boy was softened by an accumulation of birthdays.

Rumor Gal #1 "Cos ah know you has heard de news, Watha's done come back."

Rumor Gal #2 "Dey say he kilt dat man in North Carolina and went deep down in Arkansas and done de same thing there."

Rumor Gal #3 "Well, dat man Barnes brought him back cuz somebody bust him up side de head and made him almost blind."

The author points to the grave of his great-grandmother, Caroline Terry, which rests beside the grave of her oldest son, Theodore, in what was known as the "colored cemetery" in Sperryville.

Rumor Gal #1 "He betta be glad that de white man done passed away what he struck wild dat rock long long time ago."

Rumor Gal #1 "He was just playing. Ah know but he shook his fist at Cah-line and said he wanted his dinner on time. Guess what she said?"

Rumor Gal #2 "Yeah bad boy, hit may be in mind, but never will hit be in time, Laudy, dat Cah-line will never change.

To be sure, Uncle Watha, also known by the nickname "Pewter," caused no more trouble via the usual Saturday night acts that stereotyped too many individuals. Since Caroline was about 105 years old, the presence of Watha in the house with her was a relief for her daughter, Florence, who lived nearby. The main occupation of Watha was grooming the lot, cutting the underbrush and making it usable once again. The lot was approximately three-quarters of an acre, diagonally across highway 211 from where the Shaw's Service Station is located. Also he would go to the woods and cut firewood for his sister, niece, and his mother, Caroline.

In his spare time, particularly in the afternoon, he would be a regular at the Estes Mountain Store, at the checkerboard. The store was located adjacent to Estes Mill, which still stands in Sperryville along Highway 211. On the porch that extended eastward from the store, the locals gathered around the two usual combatants, Watha and Mr. Hisile, a farmer and rural mail carrier. Mr. Hisile, a learned and articulate man of reasonable means, was at a loss to explain how a man, unable to read or write, could beat him at checkers time and time again. It was amusing to listen to Uncle Watha, as he would tell Mr. Hisile to "move right along" or "come right along" and suddenly Mr. Hisile would be leaving in complete disgust with a departing remark - "Damn."

One more tragedy befell Caroline because of an unfortunate incident involving careless smoking. Lucy, in the process of lighting her pipe, accidentally set her dress afire. Whatever the material was, it was a disaster. The flames, quite fierce and spreading fast soon engulfed the frail figure of Lucy. Her great-grandson, Jim, happened to be nearby and threw a bucket of water on her in an effort to extinguish the flames, Lucy unfortunately perished during that night.

"Little James" or "Jeems" as he was called then, remembers walking hand in hand with his mother and grandmother carrying a lantern the two and one-half miles to see Aunt Lucy. Alone in a room without light, lay the small figure gasping for breath. Her eyes had a fixed state, she saw no one, nor heard anyone. Harry, her grandson, led the trio back into the living room. Tears and sighs of "My Lord, My Lord" were the only bits of conversation. All left to return home around 2:00 a.m. Aunt Lucy died sometime later early that morning.

Caroline was terribly upset when Watha told her that Lucy, her friend of slavery days and the last link to the past of toil, upheaval and eventual freedom had died. Great-grandson "Jeems" had become a frequent visitor to Aunt Caroline's or "Old Grandma" as she was called. As a boy of 12-14, he could see that she was greatly moved by Lucy's unfortunate passing, which might have been avoided.

Jeems tells the story of how "Old Grandma Caroline" got quite a laugh at the story of when two of the old ladies who had retired for the evening heard the loud sound of a trumpet playing the much-revered hymn "When the Saints Go Marching In." Startled, Aunt Harriet and Aunt Rhett jumped from their beds, they began to shout and dance about the room. "Don't you hear it Gabriel is blowing his horn. Oh, thank you Gabriel, I can hear it now. Oh, it's so beautiful. Go tell Caroline. Rhett, I know Caroline can hear it." Aunt Harriet, who could read, peeked out the window to see "Gabriel."

What she saw was a marching band and a banner that read "Hagenbach Wallace Circus." Both women disappointed, sat down on the edge of their beds and stared at each other. "How are they going to explain this one?" At that time large shows would travel via railroad from one engagement to the other, if it were accessible by rail. This show after an appearance in Luray traveled via truck to Sperryville enroute to Culpeper, another railhead. This early morning marching band, really a promotion stunt, stunned the villagers.

Caroline's health was a major concern by this time. Aunt Rhett stayed several nights a week to be on hand if any serious problems surfaced. Little James stayed at night when Aunt Rhett had to work late or had other things to do. The nightly ritual of preparing for bed was a carry-over of the plantation days. After sitting on the front porch watching the cars go by, Old Grandma would go inside the house, and she insisted that all blinds be closed tightly. Windows that were up came down and a stick was placed over the window to prevent it from being raised.

The lamp was turned down to its lowest point and placed on the floor. Next the high ladder-back chair was positioned between the lamp and window. Now a second check was made to make sure the shades were down and curtains drawn tightly. Last a sweater, apron, or petticoat was draped over the ladder-back chair. At this point, no light escaped and very, very little air came in.

Jeems slept on a cot near the window and "Old Grandma" slept in the big bed with several pillows propped around her. Now it was story time. Incidents of slavery days, incidents of previous weeks, were all retold. Phrases of "they said that... and then they all had on big hats... did I leave my pipe on the wash bench... No, there it is on the table where I left it." Sleep eventually came to soothe the weary eyes. Jeems would listen until he too would fall asleep. Fortunately, Jeems discovered a small air passage under the window and with the aid of a horseshoe nail enlarged the small break to admit welcome air on hot summer nights.

An old photograph shows Caroline setting on her front porch at her home in Sperryville sometime in the 1930's. Directly across the lot from her home was a restaurant called Celeste Café. The restaurant at that time was segregated as by law and custom. Nickelodeons were making their impact on the listening public. The sounds of summer included such tunes as "Corrine, Corrine", "You Are My Sunshine", and "Guitar Rag." In the evenings, Caroline, Aunt Rhett and the great-grandson, Jeems, would sit on the porch and enjoy the concert of the twelve selections available be played and played again. Caroline now had sight and sound to help her while away the hours of the day. Her daughter, Florence, lived just across the small Thornton River and had access by a foot bridge that was anchored on one end to a large tree so that it would be used again in case high water washed it from its moorings or base.

For the visitors who came to see her, she was Aunt Caroline, to some she was called Sis-tah Cah-line, and of course, to her family as Mama or Old Grandma. She was a determined, feisty individual even at 107 years old. One afternoon she directed Jeems to fill the washtub for her and get the homemade soap from the storage shed. After this preparation, she sought out sheets, pillowcases, aprons, and was in the process of giving them a vigorous scrubbing when Aunt Rett appeared on the scene. "Laudy, Sis-tah Cah-line what in the world are you doing?

"What does it look like ahm doing?" replied Caroline.

Concerned that the old woman was over-working herself, Aunt Rhett said, "Sis-tah Cah-line, will you please, mam, put that washboard down."

Caroline, holding her beloved pipe in one hand and the other on the board said, "Sister Rhett, will you please, mam, jes kiss my ass."

With that, Aunt Rhett responded, "Oh, Cah-line don't you see dat young boy dere?"

Caroline resumed her task at the washboard and replied, "Now jes who was I talking to, the young man or the old woman?"

Jeems and Aunt Rhett walked around the side of the house to the front porch, again the music from the across the lot came through loud and clear. "Corrine, Corrine, where have you been so long?" Aunt Rhett shook her head and said, "Ain't no use, that Cah-line is Cah-line forever."

Nannie, Caroline's youngest daughter, came home to stay in the new house she had built near her mother's home. Another daughter, Jennie, would stop by to see also this wonderful lady called Sis-tah Cah-line.

As Jeems recalls, Caroline would often say, "Isn't it remarkable, here I am way over one hundred years old and still have six children to come and see me."

This narrative would not be complete without the last story and perhaps the most laughable one: Aunt Jennie's straight and narrow flight from danger.

In Madison County there was a beautiful picnic area called Coleman's Grove. Large shade trees and plenty of parking spaces marked this favorite spot of the Sunday school set.

Not a cloud in the sky, not scorchy hot, just the ideal weather for Sunday school. Frank and Aunt Jennie came, also, Deacon Johnson and family. However, two other individuals came, both fully armed and eager to settle an old score that began a couple of years earlier in Philadelphia. One man, named Carter, and the other unknown came to get even because of a severe beating inflicted on the other years earlier. Uncle Frank and Aunt Jennie brought lots of delicious food and had just spread them on the ground at the side of their brand new Model T Ford. Fifty or more feet away, Deacon Johnson and Mrs. Johnson also had a similar display of fried pies, chocolate cake, roast beef, ham, pink lemonade and other ingredients

In back of his home on the hill overlooking the village of Sperryville, James Russell has erected a memorial to many slaves who were buried nearby. The message on his sign reads: "Memorial Hill - Approximately 2,500 ft. southwest of this site is the final resting place of 75 to 100 slaves who labored on these very grounds, 1810-1865."

for family dining.

The inevitable occurred, the two men of evil intent, suddenly saw each other, guns were drawn and shots rang out as the two men sought to end this long simmering feud. Aunt Jennie, visibly alarmed, frightened at the sight of two men in full view firing at each other decided that distance was the only avenue for safety. Aunt Jennie got a firm grip on her long skirt and was up and away. It is a known fact that a straight line is the shortest distance between two points. But what about poor Deacon Johnson whose picnic spread now loomed as the only obstacle remaining in Aunt Jennie's mad dash? Her tiny feet shod in new button shoes, she was now only a few feet away from an impromptu meeting with Deacon Johnson and family. The first step dislodged two delicious fried pies; very carefully, she avoided the roast beef, but the chocolate cake suffered terribly. Aunt Jennie made a mid-course correction after the cake encounter and was now headed toward the exit bolstered by a mighty burst of speed.

Deacon Johnson leapt up and said, "What in the h… was that?"

"Daddy, Daddy, today is Sunday," one of the children said in an effort to calm her father.

Mrs. Johnson, equally surprised, remarked, "At least she left the string beans and the roast beef untouched." Uncle Frank, trying to figure out which direction his wife took, began calling out, "Mother, Mother, did anyone see where she went?" One man laughed and said, "I have no idea, but some lady left in a heck of a hurry toward the exit gate." Another said, "I would say at her speed, she's now approaching J.E.R. Lightfood's in Culpeper. Ha Ha."

Uncle Frank offered to pay Deacon Johnson for damages, but the two after a few minutes conversation all were laughing at this impromptu meeting. For years to come this story was one good for laughs whatever the occasion was. "Old Grandma" was forever smiling and laughing when it was mentioned. "How did she learn or who did she take this speed after?" She remembered for a second or two of a run made on a cow path long, long ago on her first plantation.

In the spring of 1941 the toll of years began to manifest itself with the decline of Caroline's usual zest for living. No longer did she take her place on the porch for concert listening or just watching the cars go by. For the latter part of the month of June she became bedridden, too weak to even feed herself. Nannie, her youngest daughter, came home to look after or help in the last days. Questions came from throughout the community. How is Sis-tah Cah-line...? What's new with Mrs. Caroline Terry...? Is she in the hospital?

Her last nourishment was a cool taste of water via saturated cloth held by the baby, Nannie. On July 12, 1941, with two daughters and a granddaughter at her bedside, Caroline after enjoying a long life of 108 years passed to her eternal rest. She was now in the Fraternity of the Silent, joining so many who had preceded her. There was Suki, Drucilla, Lucy and of course, Joshua, the lad who would go like the wind that spring evening in 1833. One thought somewhat says it all.

Thou go not, like a Quarry - slave at night.
Scourged to his dungeon, but, sustained and soothed
By an unfaltering trust, approach thy grave,
Like one who wraps the drapery of his couch
about him, and lies down to pleasant dreams.
From the poem Thanatopsis

To the Readers, I trust this short chronicle of one endearing individual has been a source of understanding, entertainment and to a degree an intimate glance into what happened during those historic but unfortunate days. To the beautiful memory, I am thankful for the blessing of listening to, for the tolerance and patience of my having asked so many questions and for not being reprimanded for trying to eavesdrop on grown-up conversations. We read of incidents, we see pictures of incidents of that period in history, however, it is a true blessing to sit, hold hands and touch in person a loved one and relive the days that people still talk about.

Thank you "Old Grandma" for sharing your blessing of longevity with your great-grandson "Jeems" a.k.a. "The one who also ran."

Only a few months before she died, I wrote a little poem of tribute, which was printed in our school newspaper, the MIS Booster. The clipping, which I still have, is dated March 1941, and the headline on the poem reads: "Aunt Caroline Talks of Olden Days." It is reproduced here, just as it appeared then:

I'se been sitting here by dis winder
A-thinking and looking in de space,
Ob de service I ust to render
On old Marse plantation place.
I ust to wo'k long and hard
In those hot toilsome days
An' wonder if there was a God
That would allow such wicked ways.
I wo'ked as a slave for Marse Rhine
With my brothers and sister too,
An' sang hymns all de time,
For there was nothing to do.
I remember once how near death I came

While cooking for the Yankee men
That was to take part in the war game
To rid this ole world of sin.
A Yankee was walking by the pool,
Laughing and talking all de time,
Of religion, churches and school
That he had left behind.
And then he began to fall
Landin' head long in the pool,
I laughed, so did Marse and Mistress, all
At this young Yankee fool.
At me he raised his gun
And threatened to seal my doom,
If not Marse had stopped the fun
And sent me to my room.
So, Little James, now you see
My life has been one of toil,
Yet God has spared me
A broken body, but soul unsoiled.
So as I sit with thoughts of old,
Nothing else in this life to do.
Remember what I have told you,
Pray for me, and I for you.

Composed in honor of Mrs. Caroline Terry who was born a slave and is now living at age of 108 in Sperryville, VA.

By Little James.

PART FIVE:
THE BARBER, FARMER, JEWELER AND ENTREPRENEUR

The memory of James Arthur Engham shall forever be a source of strength and inspiration to me. His lifetime achievements reflect the story of how one determined black man faced the harsh difficult era and prevailed. The story begins in the year 1858, and moves fast forward to the year of his death on August 16, 1935.

At an early age "J. A." displayed such ingenuity and intellect that he amazed and captivated his contemporaries during the post-civil war days. The length of the work day with its dead-end hours led him to declare. "There must be a better way." As the story goes, while in the fields with fellow laborers under a merciless July sun, he suddenly dropped his grime-laden hoe and retired his sore, blistered hands to his cabin home, never looking back. Enter now at this point, the watch repairman and tonsorialist.

As he continued to work at his new vocation, he added another dimension, that of photographer. Everyone seemed to be obsessed with picture taking. Along the way, he acquired a professional camera outfit, tripod, and framer and within minutes was able to furnish his customer/subject with a beautiful personal picture. Camp meetings and church suppers

This tintype portrait of James Arthur Engham, the author's grand-father, shows the Sperryville entrepreneur in the prime of his adult years.

proved to be a booming business for the new photographer. As an added novelty he sold necklaces, beads, pins, watches, etc., to adorn the beautiful ladies, anxious to show how they looked in pictures. Demand and popularity grew by leaps and bounds. Soon a horse and buggy was needed to accommodate his growing business.

This experience of personal achievement helped prepare him for his entry into the arena of his greatest triumph--real estate. Early into the year of 1881, "J.A." made his first venture in real estate, at the age of twenty-three. Thus began an odyssey that brought him respect, admiration, and envy over a span of many years to come.

"J.A." did stop to evaluate his priorities, and discovered that a helpmate was next in order. After a quiet courtship, he won the hand of a beautiful young lady of twenty-one years, who would remain at his side for the remainder of his life. Reverend R. H. Carey, the third pastor of Hopewell Baptist Church, united James A. Engham and Florence Terry in holy matrimony on March 26, 1890. Three girls were born of this union, Roberta, Fannie, and Clara. Tragically, Clara passed at the young age of eighteen in 1917.

One of his real estate acquisitions included a grist mill called the "Old Totten Mill" located along Lee Highway (Route 211 today) just west of the village. It was extremely pleasing to a boy of eight. The building also housed a soft drink bottling business, operated by Mr. Stroll. My childhood travels of the day invariably took me by the old mill to watch the bottling process and to sample the tasty strawberry Try-Me drink. Much later, I learned about the source of its base ingredient, water. A question now, but delight then. The operator of the gristmill was a white haired gentleman nicknamed "Coly". Quite capable in his profession, he kept the stones honed/sharpened to perfection. Many, many, farmers brought their grain to the mill to be ground for their use. The pond in the winter months furnished enough ice for family use during the summer. This mill continued operation until the 1930's.

Near the large house where "J.A." lived, on Main Street in Sperryville, was his own personal electric power plant. This furnished power to three houses he owned and one other building. Delco Power was a very up-to-date electric source, with its rows and rows of batteries and alcohol/kerosene-powered generator.

One unforgettable episode began with a simple task given me by "J.A.", as I recall in the fall of 1927. I rode with "J.A." to

J.A. Engham, his wife Florence and children, stand out front of the Sperryville home on Main Street where he lived and conducted business as a jeweler, barber and real estate investor. Note the striped barber pole on the right.

a small orchard, located near the site of the Blue Moon Restaurant. I got out of the Graham Touring car, with its snap-on, Eisen glass windows. I was given an empty 12-pound flour sack with Fletcher's Mill printed on its front. I was told to gather a bag of golden delicious apples for a Mr. Hisle while he and "J.A" talked. In my eagerness to return and listen in on the conversation, my choice of apples ranged from ripe, over-ripe, rabbit selected, to whatever was within easy reach.

My grandfather scolded me for such an unwise choice of undesirable selections. He looked at me and thus began a lesson that reverberates even today. "I would like to live long enough, just to see what you are going to do in later life. Are you going to gather the bad apples, when you have an absolute opportunity to gather the good ones?"

The most pleasant childhood experience was the opportunity to ride with "J.A." in his new 1929 Hupmobile. Twin spare tires were mounted on either side of the motor, and the car could do sixty miles an hour. Also free wheel at a breathtaking speed. The colored folks came to see Mr. Engham's car, but the folks of other ethnic backgrounds came to see Uncle Arthur's car. But they all came. For a man of color, that could pay $950.00 cash for a car in 1929 was an unbelievable feat. To ride in this luxurious vehicle was a childhood delight.

During his lifetime with his inseparable partner, Florence, "J.A." became involved in the sale and purchase of over 32 pieces of real estate, including the gristmill, seven houses, and several farm properties totaling approximately 200 acres.

Seven area homeowners owe their initial success at becoming landowners to the very Christian and liberal consideration by the heirs and widow of "J.A." estate. Which by some comparison, was like buying land on a lay-a-way plan. One local man, after being disabled in a farming accident, sold apples on the roadside and earned enough to purchase a lot from Mrs. Florence Engham. I recall watching the smiling face of Mr. Gaylord Butler as he counted out sixty-one dollar bills to my grandmother and in a never-ending smile declared, "Aunt Florence, I do believe this just about makes it." The purchase was recorded some days later and Mr. Butler became a landowner for the first time.

The large house on Main Street where "J.A." had his watch repair shop and jewelry display still stands in the heart of Sperryville. Gone now is the tall barber pole, the huge display watch, and the engraving machine, and the sights and sound of a busy time in the flourishing days of 1908 through 1935. No more is the aroma of lilac water, shaving cream and spicy cigar smoke. Silent now is the sound of several chiming clocks; the warm glow of a pot-bellied coal stove and the hos-

The J.A. Engham home still stands on Main Street in Sperryville, with an attached addition. In this photo, James Russell stands by a small display case honoring Mr. Engham.

pitality of that small town setting. All is now etched into history by the cold, impersonal winds of time.

During the early morning hours of August 16, 1935, "J.A." departed this life with his family at his bedside. A newspaper account of J.A.'s passing listed him as one of the wealthiest colored men in Rappahannock County. Today, one grandson, after leaving the military service went on to be a printer at the Government Printing Office in Washington, D.C. After later serving as a consultant with a large printing company in Washington, D.C., he is now retired. The other grandson is still pondering the apple gathering decision. No more apples, no more trees, but the lesson of that episode will remain with me always.

PART SIX:
UNCLE THEODORE AND 'JEEMS'

The year was 1933, probably during the early days of April. The days inspired the local folks to be just plain happy to feel the warm breeze as it drifted from the mountains. Everyone embraced the warmth of the breeze at it gently caressed the faces of adults and children alike. The years 1931 through 1933 had been a tortuous period. The winters were cruel, that which lent an affinity to an economic depression that was sweeping the land. However, the promises of President Franklin D. Roosevelt brought new life into the small community of Sperryville, Virginia.

Jeems and his great uncle, Theodore, sat on the porch of Aunt Nannie's house. At the time, Aunt Nannie was working in New York for a very rich family that was involved in the import/export business.

Jeems was eager to show Uncle Thea the Ralston Six Shooter pistol, a wooden replica of the old western guns. This treasure had just arrived in the mail. Boy! How long Jeems had waited for that gun, even after mailing the labels from the Purina food boxes, along with 25¢. The fee so patiently saved had helped prepare Jeems for the long awaited day the "straight shooter" would finally arrive, which seemed like forever.

There in the gathering dusk of a Saturday evening, two individuals sat in unison of old and young. One was listening and enjoying the nostalgia of youth, the other ambling on with the effervescence of imagination.

"Jeems, did I ever tell you about the time I helped track down that hoss thief?" Attention now departed the six-shooter and was now focused on Uncle Thea's adventure. "Yes, sir! I was right there with the posse and them others, Jeems, before I tell you about it, I want you to do me a favor. I generally gits me an appetizer from "Big Charlie" on Saturday evenings. Could you go over and get me a bottle for it gets any later? I also specs since that gun of yours look so real you can just leave it with me so nobody will think you came over to shoot up the town."

Jeems in his eagerness to accommodate his great uncle, strode off toward the parking spot of "Big Charlie", Jeems in his bib overalls, tattered and worn, sporting a 1930 version of the African bush hairstyle and wearing tennis shoes of extended use. Jeems pondered how he would approach Mr. Charlie. "Hi, Mister Charlie, are you the Medicine Man? You got any Lip-Lap on you? I got the money if you have the dise (merchandise)." At 12 years, Jeems wanted to sound grown up, but nothing sounded right.

As he approached the 1930 Ford of Mr. Charlie, a booming voice sounded off. "Hey, boy, you want something?" The rehearsed approach became lost in the face-off between a 300 lb. white man and a somewhat frightened 12-year-old colored youth buying moonshine for the first time. "Er, Suh, Uncle Theodore said here is 50¢ and to send him something." The tension was broken when he replied, "al'right, hand it here."

The Ford sedan contained his wife in the front seat and two very plump daughters in the back. "Ella, hand me a bottle here for that boy. By the way, ain't that Rob Russell's boy?"

The transaction now completed, Jeems tucked the warm bottle in his bib overalls just as he had seen the grown-up do. The bottle was very warm indeed. Well, it lent credence to the story of the merchandise being transported unseen in the voluminous bloomers of the agents in the rear seat of the car. They sat on bottles as well, and hid them secretly in their clothing.

The purchase completed, Uncle Theodore now breathed a sigh of relief as Jeems handed him the brown bottle of the highly potent appetizer. "Here Jeems, take a taste, it won't hurt you, it will make you feel better." Jeems accepted his uncle's invitation, thus he gained an unforgettable evening.

Two individuals, one in complete contentment, the other younger, in confusion and bewilderment. The warm potent medicine now exerted an exhilaration of new and unfamiliar dimension. Theodore enjoyed a comfortable and reassuring feeling. For Jeems, the end of the porch for some unknown reason gradually appeared to rise and sway in the moon-drenched countryside.

"Go ahead, Jeems, take another smile, it's ok you are almost home." (Reason was lost in that flushed and unique moment of complete abandon) Uncle Thea said it was OK but why was the porch continuously moving? Jeems now felt that need for some sanctuary from the unfamiliar turmoil. Perhaps if he went over and sat on "Old Grandma's" porch this feeling of uneasiness would disappear. Enroute, the short familiar path was totally now winding. The picket fence nearby became uncomfortingly close. Suddenly the path sprang into an upright position. "Not so!" Jeems was looking downward toward the sanctuary of "Old Grandma's" porch.

Minutes grew into approximately two hours. The porch

regained its stability. The picket fence moved to its former position and remained so. The euphoria of the early evening left a bitter taste, an unusual headache, and of course a lesson well learned. Children should listen only and not try to imitate or act out the adult behavior until they in due time become adults themselves.

Twenty years later, Uncle Theodore's health became a serious problem. On a late Saturday evening Jeems, now a grown man, gave Uncle Thea a can of old German beer. "That sure tasted good. It's been a long time since I had anything like that."

The two men exchanged smiles. The circle was now complete: Uncle Thea gave Jeems his first drink. Jeems gave Uncle Thea his last. Two weeks later Uncle Thea passed at the age of 98 years.

PART SEVEN:
JAMES RUSSELL REMEMBERS . . . LIFE IN SPERRYVILLE

Editor's Note: In the summer of 2001, James Russell agreed to record his memories of growing up and living in Sperryville over a span of 80 years. These oral interviews were tape recorded and edited by James P. Gannon, to be included in this publication.

I was born in Sperryville on April 25, 1921. My parent's house was in Sperryville, just beyond where the Appetite Repair Shop is now. That was my birthplace. I lived there until 1937, when I completed grade school here in Sperryville. The grade school for the black kids in Sperryville was on the highway, (Route 211) directly across from the shop now known as Central Coffee Roasters. They taught all the grades in that school, which was called Sperryville Colored School. That school building has since been torn down. The school was relocated from the corner of Oventop Road and Route 211, to Route 600. This was done to provide more room and safety for the school. The black folks of Sperryville purchased one acre of land (on Route 600) from C.E. "Ned" Johnson. (That school building still stands there today, just up the road from the restaurant, Appetite Repair Shop.)

I started school in 1927 when I was six years old. We walked to school, about a mile-and-a-half. Other black kids had much longer distances to travel, up to three or four miles, from down in FT Valley. There was a family named Jackson down there with a horse and buggy. When the Jackson kids were being taken to school, it was fun for us to run and catch a ride on the back of the buggy. In those days there was no public transportation for the black children in school.

When I was in school, we had 25 to 30 kids in seven grades-first grade through seventh. You would go to high school after seventh grade. There were several teachers I

The Sperryville Colored School, shown here in a photo taken about 1915, was attended by children in the first through seventh grade. The one-room school originally was located at the corner of Oventop Road and Lee Highway (Route 211). In 1933, a lot was purchased from Waltom Wood on Route 600, to which the building was moved to provide a safer location.

remember. There was H.R. Russell, who was my father, Bertie M. Stafford, and a Mr. Pleasant. Also there was a Maggie McKeever, all of these were black teachers. Our supplies for the school came from the white high school in Sperryville. At that time, the white high school was located at the corner of Route 522 and Route 211. As the books were updated at the white school, those that were discarded came to us.

Water for our school came from a spring at Estes Mill. We loved that place for a number of reasons. It was a sort of a lark for two boys or girls to take a 10-quart pail and go up and get water from the spring. We loved to go up there because Estes Mill had a store, Estes Mountain Store. They

The schoolhouse where James Russell and the black children of Sperryville attended classes still stands, rather weather-beaten and unused, on Route 600 on the hills above the old village. This building was dismantled and relocated to the Route 600 site from its prior location along the highway, now Route 211, not far from Estes Mill.

had cheese and crackers that we could buy for pennies. They also had horehound candy, very tasty. Another thing was the sodas. There was a local bottler that lived in the Sperryville area that supplied drinks called "Try Me." Strawberry was my preference. To go up to the Mill for water was a double treat for us. It was a break from being in class, and an opportunity to buy candy and sodas.

I think I got a fair education there. The teachers were sincere. They taught as well as their preparation allowed. But the books--there was one particular book I remembered, and still wonder about now. It was a story and some pictures of some "pickaninnies" dancing around a campfire. The caption was,

Estes Mill stands outside the village of Sperryville along the Thornton River, which once provided water to drive its grinding wheels. James Russell stands beside the stone foundation that supported the Estes Mountain Store. An old spring next to the store provided buckets of water that the black school children would fetch from here, where they would stop for a treat of candy or crackers from the store.

"Happy slave children dancing around the campfire." The question has always lingered with me: "Where do you find these happy slaves?" But this is what we had at the time. We had McGuffey's readers. We had geography, civics, arithmetic, the basics.

Bertie May Stafford was a teacher of note. She had a master's degree from the University of Indiana. She was a teacher's teacher-very well prepared, capable. She attracted the admiration, as well as the envy, of all the local teachers here, black and white. There was a white teacher here and my uncle overheard a conversation between her and some local people. They asked, "What do you think of that black teacher up there, Bertie May Stafford?" And her reply was, "Well, I don't know. I like her and I don't like her. I don't like no black nigger over top of me." She meant that the black teacher had a degree higher than she had. Those were her words.

In those years, as a young black child, I felt alienated, outcast, subhuman. Why? For example, going to school, we walked while the other kids rode. The white kids spit out the window of the bus, threw spitballs at us, or whatever projectiles they had. I wondered, what was wrong with me? Why do I have to walk? Those were the ideas that were in my mind then because of the social status of blacks. In one word, I felt alienated.

Our parents and teachers dealt with that by teaching us to become the best. My father was a teacher for 33 years. Learn, absorb, and demonstrate that you are capable, as capable as the other person. Don't ever think that because of your racial background that you are not capable as a human being, or as other persons. You have the capacity to do, to develop and produce, given a level playing ground. Just because the back of the bus was your lot, it still didn't mean that you were inferior. It was the social system of the time; it was the law of the land.

In my growing up in Sperryville, I shall never forget my four playmates - all white boys - that lived on the hill across the roadway from my house. Felton, Winifred, Alvin Lewis and Herbert will always be a part of that recollection of the 1930s. They evoked laughter, confrontation, and an occasional fight. But at the close of the day, it was "See you tomorrow. Don't forget, tomorrow we are going to look for gold."

Let me share two childhood incidents that still have me laughing now. The gang and I set out early one morning on a fishing expedition to the Thorton river. I had the prettiest fishing pole and I caugh the largest fish. We returned home in a very vexatious mood. Probably vecause of my refusal to give up the largest fish, antagonism began to manifest itself. The boys went to their house on the hill. Then the chant of "Black Nee-gro, Black Nee-gro!" resounded down the hill. I felt puzzled. Why the name-calling? From my perch on the porch swing I went into the kitchen where my mother was preparing food. She felt that some childhood incident had come about but said nothing. After about an hour, Alvin Lewis came to the roadway near the house and called, "Aunt Bert, can James come out and play?" This was the way it was - we played, we quarrelled, but before the day was over, we were all looking forward to the next day.

Another episode that brings a smile began with a game of "follow the leader." On Route 600 at Hopewell Lane there stood an old barn where Felton decided to inaugurate the game. First, Felton took off his shirt, his pants, cap, shoes and then his underwear and hung them on the boards that enclosed the stall in the barn. We all did likewise - Winifred, Alvin Lewis, Herbert and myself.

Felton said, "Follow me!" We started in a trot towards

where now stands the Hopewell Baptist Church, then toward Frye's house and Mildred Butler's house. There were no houses on the grounds at that time. But just for imagination, can you visualize four white boys and one colored boy running nude that distance across the hill? A sight to behold, indeed! We all dressed hurriedly and ran home. This beyond a shadow of a doubt deserved an X-rated label!

I have recently learned that Alvin Lewis, Felton and Winifred are no longer with us to recall that episode. Herbert, the only living one of my original playmates, now lives somewhere near Winchester, Virginia.

Another unforgettable day for me was Election Day 1932, for I became a celebrant in a victory dance not of my own choosing, to say the least. At that time, Oakley Hopkins operated a blacksmith shop in Sperryville, one of three operating during that era. I was eleven years old at the time, turning the bellows at Oakley's shop that sunny morning when three "mountain hoogies" rode in, quite drunk. "Mountain hoogie" was the term applied to folks living in and beyond the Beech Spring area; they were proud, hostile and had limited or no education. One of them exclaimed loudly, "Well, Oakley, I see you have a real black smith here. Ha, Ha, a little black smith. I bet that boy can dance, too. Go ahead, boy, cut a little step. Let us see you dance!"

"No, sir," I responded, "I am not a good dancer at all. See here, these soles have come loose and they go flap, flap, all the time." Oakley unsuccessfully implored the drunken trio to leave his help alone, as he needed someone to turn the bellows for his forge. But his pleas went unheeded.

"Dammit, nigger, if I have to get down off this hoss...you see this whip? By George, you are going to do something!" So I started to perform, in an ever-widening circle. Flap, flap went my Depression shoes. Scared feet, tired feet, eager to vacate the premises. Then the men laughed and slapped their sides and said, "Didn't I tell you all them coon niggers could dance?" I glanced at the men, who were in near hysterics then, and took off running - flap, flap went the shoes, but each flap took me farther away from that ordeal. I can laugh now at one of the many episodes that characterized the 1930s.

One must remember that this was a time of Depression, and a shortage of consumer goods. Bolts of cloth were sold in the store's dry-good department by the yard, as a lot of local women made their own dresses and aprons. Not too many people had finances to buy homes, or even to rent except that which was at the low end of the totem pole. I remember a conversation between two former slaves - Richard Holmes Sr., and Daniel Aylor, both veterans of the plantation era. They compared the merits of the slavery system of allotments against the struggles and the doles of the Depression. Slaves were allotted so many pounds of flour, so many pounds of meat, and so on, per year. Now, there was no guarantee of either in Depression days.

Sperryville had industry in those days. There was "the evaporator," a place for drying and processing apples. Apples were machine-washed, peeled, sliced and placed on trays to go into the heating ovens to extract moisture. The Hitt planing mill was another place of industry in Sperryville. Lumber was brought into the mill for finishing into floors, cabinets or anything that required a smooth finish. The Hitts also made wagon wheels, parts for wagons, caskets, and in fact they had a burial service, with horse-drawn carriages. The Hitt family purchased that business from the Kiger family. Kiger was a builder of the famed Conestoga Wagon that traveled the Western plains. My grandmother lived next door (on Main

Street) to the Hitts, and it was a childhood delight for me to peer through the white picket fence to watch C.C. Lewis start the gasoline engine - a single-cylinder affair which made a very loud noise with its chug-chug-bang-bang sound, as it powered the milling machines.

As part of the NRA program (National Recovery Act, a Depression jobs program of President Franklin D. Roosevelt), a sewing room was located on Main Street, in a large room which is now the home of Elizabeth Lee Harris. This sewing room was headed by Mrs. Estelle Dodson, who was wheel-chair bound, but quite capable of directing the several women who made uniforms and such for various government agencies. A Civilian Conservation Corps camp was located west of

James Russell grew up in this home in Sperryville in the years before World War II, and returned to live here after retiring from his job as a mail carrier in Washington, D.C. in 1980.

Sperryville on the grounds of what is now the Hearthstone School. This provided employment as well as instruction in the basic skills of reading and writing.

Believe it or not, there was more than one grocery store in Sperryville at that time. E.M. Schwartz owned and operated what is now the Sperryville Corner Store. James Estes had two stores - the town store, then located where the Post Office now stands, and the Mountain Store, west of town on Route 211 where Estes Mill still stands. Another small retailer was Jake Atkins. He had a gas pump and a nickelodeon that blared out "Guitar Rag" again and again. His son, nicknamed Gray Eyes, operated an eatery just south of the store on Route 211, called the Celeste Cafe. Also working there were Mr. Curtis and daughter Mary Ellen, Mrs. John Powell Jenkins and daughter "We-We". It was small but popular to the local gentry and an oasis for the tourist traffic coming to the new Skyline Drive in the 1935-37 era.

Sperryville also had a drug store operated by William E. Jarrell, diagonally across from the Post Office. He sold medicine, prescriptions, ice cream, and Victrola needles for the old crank-up record players. The 78-RPM records by colored artists such as Pine Top Smith, Duke Ellington and Louis Armstrong were called Race Records, and could be ordered through the Montgomery Ward or Sears Roebuck catalogues.

Near the bridge over the Thornton River where the Appetite Repair Shop is today was a grocery store operated by Clyde Atkins. This building housed the post office, where stamps sold for three cents. The postmaster was John Powell Jenkins, a holdover from Hoover days. The Atkins store was a great hangout when it aired the Joe Louis vs. Max Schmeling fights on radio in 1936. Not too many locals had radios, so it was a gathering spot, with the white folks inside and the colored at the end of a long porch.

After finishing seventh grade, I went to what was known then as the Manassas Regional High School. At that time, there were no provisions for black high school students in Rappahannock County. The nearest school that we had at that time was in Manassas. It was also called the Manassas Industrial School.

They had a boarding department, and the kids stayed on the campus. I was there boarding from February of 1938, until graduation with the Class of 1941. While I was boarding there, I would come home only on holidays--if transportation was available. Manassas was about 60 miles away. I would come home for Thanksgiving, Christmas, Easter - but beyond that I remained on the campus. It was a growing-up experience. Here you were thrown into association with kids of different backgrounds, some who came from the DC area. Some were talented, some very capable, some smart and some not so smart.

My studies included printing. We set type by hand. We didn't have any Linotype machines. We picked the letters from the case and put them into the composing stick to form the words. We put them on the job press and printed our newspaper, the MIS Booster. I was the editor of the MIS Booster. I still have some copies of it.

The school had both academic subjects and trades classes. Originally, an ex-slave by the name of Jennie Dean started the Manassas school. She saw the need for instructions for black kids. She solicited funds from the Carnegie Foundation and others. It was called the Manassas Industrial School because of the idea of preparing students for the trades. For the boys there was a bricklaying department, a masonry department, a printing department and building trades. For the girls there was home economics--food preparation, ironing, and what have you.

Later on it became known as the Manassas Regional High School. Up to 1937, it was supported solely by donated funds. In 1937, the director was William H. Barnes--we called him "Workhorse Barnes" - originally from North Carolina. Under his directorship, support came mainly from state funds. Now, the kids who attended school from Rappahannock were given some money from Rappahannock County, because there was no place for them to go to school here. The county funds went directly to the school. During the summer months, the students worked on the campus. The school had a diary farm and the kids worked on the farm to help defray the cost of their attending. I graduated on May 30, 1941. Out of a class of 79, I was the class president, fourth out of 79. That was sixty years ago.

As for family, I had one sister. My sister has been dead for over 50 years. She passed April 11, 1951. My mother passed away in 1973, and my father on June 11, 1954. That's 47 years, 50 years and 28 years that I have been without close family.

There were certain restrictions on land purchases. It was not expected that we would buy in this area of town (referring to Main Street); we bought back off the road. We did trade at the local stores, because there was no choice. But we stood at the end of the counter, and we waited for the person who was the designated customer. For example, I remember C.C. Lewis told me he went into the store and was looking at a bolt of cloth. Then another person came in, and the storeowner said, "Well, you are not in a hurry, are you? I'll wait on the other person." Well, what are you going to say? No, you can't be in a hurry. It was the custom.

The same thing happened during rationing during World War II. Meat and cigarettes were rationed. My father went into the store, and saw a cut of meat and sought to purchase it. He was told, "Robert, that is already sold. That is already asked for." Then a white person came in and saw the meat, and said, "Oh, I see you have this meat today," and she got it. It had not been sold, but it was reserved for whites.

In 1936, Joe Louis fought Max Schmeling. At that time, not everyone could afford the luxury of a radio and very few blacks could. So we stood on the porch of the store, which at that time was opposite where the Appetite Repair Shop is now. It was a long, red store and post office staffed by Clyde Atkins. The blacks stood on the porch while everyone else was inside. But we could hear the radio because they had it up loud.

We listened to it. In the first fight, Schmeling beat Joe Louis. There was jubilation among the whites. They loved it. When they came out, everyone was smiling and laughing. The blacks returned home very quietly. The next morning, there was a gentleman who lived near me, and he called across to his neighbor: "Well, we've gotten rid of the nigger." That gives you an idea of the mood of the people. I had no idea that so much feeling could be engendered among the people on such a situation.

After the second fight when Joe Louis beat Schmeling, things were the exact opposite. The whites were quiet, very subdued. As Schmeling was defeated, they felt defeated. We didn't say anything until we got down the road, and then we could holler. But we waited till we got down the road. These are situations that I experienced that were reflective of the mood of the community during that time.

The number of blacks here now is very small, but at that time there were quite a number of black families. One of the large employers of the blacks was the Miller Dairy owned by Clifford Miller. He had a number of tenant houses down where the (electrical) power plant is now, along Water Street. That area was called "Fishtown," down along the river. There were about six houses with black families. They worked for Miller at the diary farm. He owned those houses, which have all been torn down. There were black folks that lived in Majors Hollow. This was settled by some ex-slaves. Some of them worked on the Fletcher plantation. At the close of the Civil War they remained in the area.

After graduation from high school on May 30, 1941, I went to went to Washington D.C. and began to work there in a restaurant called the Executive Drug Store. They had a lunch counter there. It was on 17th and K Streets. I made a total of $18 a week. It was beautiful money then. It was more than I had ever earned in Rappahannock. I worked there until September of 1941 and at that time I began my studies at Hampton Institute. I was on a work-study program; I worked four hours a day and attended classes four hours a day. While I was at Hampton I always worked. I recall I was working at a bowling alley in Phoebus, Va. It had an unholy name, because it was a stopping place for the sailors - but I won't go into detail on that.

I was working at the bowling alley in Phoebus on the evening of December 7, 1941. A newsboy came running through with the papers announcing, "Japanese Planes Bomb Pearl Harbor!" Everybody was scrambling to get the newspaper, and he sold out very quickly. Later on, we listened to the news, and heard President Roosevelt talk about the "Day of Infamy." I will never forget that, and then the next day was the declaration of war. Some of my fellow classmates and I spoke about how the die had been cast, and we wondered what will happen now? Will we see each other again? It was my freshman year at Hampton Institute, and I was enrolled in the printing department. In the spring of 1942, I went to Washington and started working in the munitions building on 19th and Constitution Avenue, NW. I worked there until 1943, at which time I entered the service. I worked there in what was called the War Department Post Office, which handled the mail between different agencies, such as the Navy Department, Air Corps, and so on. At that time there were many temporary buildings that sprang up.

One of the highlights of my time at Hampton was the time I had the honor to escort the First Lady of the Land, Mrs. Eleanor Roosevelt. She came to our school visiting, and I don't know why I was chosen - but I was - to show her the department where the printing class did its work. I showed her the Linotype machine, the Ludlow, and a printing press called the Miehle Vertical. I remember her saying, "You are doing very well, aren't you?" and she encouraged me to continue my education. I liked her. I will always remember her, and that is 60 years ago. I will always remember being encouraged by the First Lady of the Land, Mrs. Roosevelt. That was a highlight of my life.

I entered the military on March 1, 1943. I was the corporal in charge of a group of four or five black kids who left Sperryville at that time to join the Army. We all boarded a bus together on Main Street in Sperryville out in front of the hotel. The group of us arrived some hours later at Fort George Meade, Maryland. We went from Fort George Meade to Fort Huachuca in Arizona. As I recall, it was a Tuesday when we left Fort George Meade, and arrived by train at Fort Huachuca on Saturday. The train took a rather winding route, due to security. When we arrived at Fort Huachuca, it was very hot. They said it was "90 miles from Phoenix, 45 miles from Douglas, and 10 miles from H-E-L-L." This was the description we had of Fort Huachuca. It was a desert climate-very cool at night, very hot in the day.

I was assigned to the 37th Special Services Company. I always get a laugh out of this, because it was not exactly a combat outfit. It was a support unit that took care of the recreational needs of the soldiers. The combat soldiers called the special services company "the bastard child of the Red Cross and the Salvation Army." So it was another unholy

James Russell in uniform during his Army days during World War II.

name we had. I was trained as a motion picture projectionist. I learned to operate a 16-millimeter projector. We were assigned to the 92nd Division, which was in training at Fort Huachuca. We left for overseas in March of 1944. We boarded a ship and were nine days en route to French Morocco, North Africa. In mid-1944 we were transferred to Sardinia, and after a brief stay there, we went to Corsica, and then to Naples, Italy, and later to Genoa.

While we were overseas, our duty was to provide recreation to the combat troops as they came from the battle areas. All of the men in our unit were black. There were about 100 men in the company.

There were some black combat soldiers. But at that time, it was the opinion of those higher up that there was some doubt about the blacks' ability to perform as a combat soldier. Major General Edward Almond was the commanding general of the 92nd Division, and he had some doubt about black soldiers in combat. Why? It was a carryover from the social structure of the American society at the time. At the outset of the war, there was no provision for black volunteers from our area. There were a number of blacks from Rappahannock County who intended to volunteer, but there were no provisions for black volunteers from this area. I believe they sent them down to Georgia or some place where there was a high concentration of blacks.

One of the most distracting and discouraging things happened during our stay in Italy. During the time that the infantry regiments of the 92nd Division were engaged in combat, there was an article in Time magazine, which read, "Despite the efforts of the War Department to give the Negro an opportunity to conduct himself as a soldier, he has proved to be a dismal failure." I close my eyes when I say this, because when I close my eyes, I can see it. That was very, very upsetting and demoralizing to the soldiers. How are you going to encourage any kind of patriotic duty or performance if you have been labeled as a failure to begin with? This was in Time magazine! I read it myself. I do remember those lines. That was 56 years ago. In our camp one night, there was a black lieutenant, and his reconnaissance group was in the area. He came to our tent. He was a very intelligent person, a 2nd lieutenant. We talked with him. It affected his performance. I recall looking him in the eye, and him saying, "How and why am I supposed to be doing this reconnaissance on the enemy when the War Department says I am a dismal failure?" I remember that night.

There was a guy named John Reddy who was a tall, Indian-looking guy. He and I and a white soldier we were out talking, one night in Naples. The German planes came over and dropped a flare, which illuminated the area as if it was day. The German plane was taking pictures. Immediately the anti-aircraft guns started up, and I remember the three of us ran and jumped in the ditch, very close together. That was democracy at its best! The three of us--the white, the Indian guy, and myself, holding hands in the ditch.

Another thing I will forever remember was my assignment at the club at Viareggio, Italy, at the close of the war. My assignment that particular day was to go up to the club and open up the library in the morning. Adjoining this club was another building that was a storage area for unexploded shells, duds, mines and what have you, that had been collected by the soldiers. One of the workers must have dropped one of the shells or explosives, and that building blew up. The building where I was assigned also was flattened. On that particular morning, there were 36 persons hurled into eternity. They were killed - 24 soldiers from the 92nd Division, and 12 civilians. I had a friend by the name of James Gant. His outfit was assigned to search for the bodies. He told me that each body he found, he would turn it over to see if it was Russell. But I was not in that building that day. For whatever reason, I don't remember, I had missed that assignment that morning. And we laughed about it, and I said, "I am glad you didn't find me."

And now I think about that 56 years later. But for a missed assignment, I could have been among that group of 36. It would have been 37. They were all killed there. To me, the war ended there. I never did see a German soldier in combat. I do recall seeing a German soldier, a prisoner of war. I do have some souvenirs that I got from German prisoners, that I traded with them for food, C Rations and candy bars.

I was mustered out of the service on November 11, 1945. Originally, it had been planned that we would be reassigned to the Far East. But it so happened that while we were in the staging area at Naples, August 6, 1945, the atomic bomb was dropped on Hiroshima, and then Nagasaki, Japan. And that ended it. I returned to Boston in August of 1945. I came home on a two-months furlough, and then returned to Fort George Meade. There, I was discharged on a Sunday morning, November 11, 1945, with $100 in my pocket, and $200 forth-coming - a young man like a Jack Out of the Box.

I came back to Sperryville, and asked my mother to just let me rest - do nothing. I didn't do anything for two weeks. Not too much had changed in Sperryville. I remember walking up the street in my combat boots, and the people were looking at me. I don't know what impression they had of me - as a sym-bol of the combat men, or somebody who is going to come home and take their job. I always wondered what their per-ception was, and I wonder now. There wasn't a whole lot of welcome - acceptance, yes, but not welcome. There were still lynchings going on in the South.

After a respite in Sperryville, I went back to Washington, and worked at a restaurant at 2700 F Street. That was my first job after the war. In 1946, I re-entered Hampton Institute for another year. I didn't get back to Hampton in 1947, though I wanted to very, very badly. I went to Newport News, Va., and went looking for a job at night, so I could attend school. For about 10 days, the bus station was my headquarters. I went to the Veterans Administration, and I did find a job, but it would have been in the daytime, which would have prevented me from going to school. I was disappointed and came back to Washington. In 1948, I went to the Bureau of Engraving and Printing, working as a skilled helper - a glorified laborer. I stayed there for eight years, to July 16, 1956. Then I went to work for the Postal Service as a carrier, and stayed there 25 years-to November 11, 1980. That completed 35 years of government service - 25 years as a postal carrier, eight years at the Bureau of Engraving and Printing, and approximately three years as a soldier.

I retired then and came back to Sperryville. I developed what is now the Blue Moon restaurant. I was a co-owner of the Blue Moon. I lived in the home where my mother and father had lived - just up the hill from the Appetite Repair Shop. While I was still working in Washington, I built what was called the Texas Red Barbecue, at the site where Blue Moon is today. I owned that property, which I purchased in 1962 from Roberta Russell and Fanny Engham. I built this little carry-out. The carry-out mysteriously caught fire and was burned on August 27, 1975. At that time, a white Texan operated it. I reported it to the authorities. I am convinced that he deliberately set it afire. The arson squad in Culpeper was also convinced it was arson, but couldn't develop any proof.

Why? We had a piece of restaurant equipment called an updraft, which channels the heat from the cooking upward. The man who ran the restaurant wanted to move that, and I told him not to move it, because it would be a terrible risk of fire. Somehow or other, the word got to me that "he was going to move it, and he didn't have to take orders from a nigger." This was a mentality from the 1930s.

We built the building, now known as the Blue Moon, in 1980. The site had stayed vacant and overgrown with brush since 1975, when Texas Red Barbecue burned. It was an eyesore, as it was described by Mrs. Ned Johnson. It was an eyesore, because I was very discouraged and didn't attempt to do anything. But then on second thought, I realized the only one losing was James Russell. So I cleared that up, and joined with a man named Clarence Johnson, and we combined whatever resources we had and started up what was then called the Horseshoe Hills Family Restaurant.

We secured a building permit in 1980 and construction began in 1983. Clarence Johnson's brother from Florence, South Carolina, came along with a team of men and stayed at my house and they built the present structure as it is seen now. Clarence Johnson and I opened the restaurant on July 3, 1987. We operated the restaurant for a while. It was ambitious of us. You have to have ambition to do things, but you also need skill, you need know-how, you need rapport with the community, you need a whole lot of things. What was needed we didn't have. We rented the property to a restaurant operator named James T. Hartman, who operated what was called High on the Hog. At the outset, it was very good, basically a barbecue place. I don't know exactly what happened to Hartman, but he left, not under pleasant circumstances. Then it was operated by John Loretta and Chaz Green. Chaz

Green was a very good cook. From them it went to George Rosenbaum, the latest owner. And that is the story of the Blue Moon restaurant.

So that covers the history of Russell, his growing up days, with a number of omissions of course, to the present time. What does Russell do now, at 80 years, 4 months? What's next? The question is how much time does James Russell have now? That's why I was asking you this morning about a museum to show the Rappahannock of old, what the mechanics did, what the teachers did, and what others who lived here did. So I still have some ambition, but ambition is always limited by health, and by finances. What James Russell would like to do at this juncture is to see the development of a facility that would house relics and memorabilia of the early days of Rappahannock County.

The author inspects the old family Bible, believed to be the one from which Caroline learned about Scripture.

INDEX

Quick Order Form

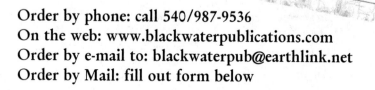

For additional copies of Beyond
the Rim by James Russell

Order by phone: call 540/987-9536
On the web: www.blackwaterpublications.com
Order by e-mail to: blackwaterpub@earthlink.net
Order by Mail: fill out form below

Name _____

Address_____

City _____ State _____Zip_____

Enclose $14.95 for each copy, plus $4 for shipping one
book, or $5 for two books. Virginia residents add 5%
sales tax ($0.75) or $15.70 per book, plus shipping.
Make check to Blackwater Publications.
Mail to: Blackwater Publications, P.O. Box 80,
Boston, VA 22713

If you want an author-signed copy, check here__✓____

**Money-back guarantee: Returnable for a full refund if
you are unsatisfied for any reason.**

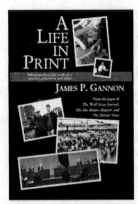